AF663811

Hands-On Monitoring and Alerting with Prometheus

Build Resilient, Real-time Monitoring and Alerting Systems using Prometheus, PromQL, and Proven Best Practices for Modern Infrastructure

Muhammad Badawy

www.orangeava.com

Copyright © 2025, Orange Education Pvt Ltd, AVA®

All rights reserved. No part of this book may be reproduced, stored in a retrieval system, or transmitted in any form or by any means, without the prior written permission of the publisher, except in the case of brief quotations embedded in critical articles or reviews.

Every effort has been made in the preparation of this book to ensure the accuracy of the information presented. However, the information contained in this book is sold without warranty, either express or implied. Neither the author nor **Orange Education Pvt Ltd** or its dealers and distributors, will be held liable for any damages caused or alleged to have been caused directly or indirectly by this book.

Orange Education Pvt Ltd has endeavored to provide trademark information about all of the companies and products mentioned in this book by the appropriate use of capital. However, **Orange Education Pvt Ltd** cannot guarantee the accuracy of this information. The use of general descriptive names, registered names, trademarks, service marks, etc. in this publication does not imply, even in the absence of a specific statement, that such names are exempt from the relevant protective laws and regulations and therefore free for general use.

First Published: June 2025

Published By: Orange Education Pvt Ltd, AVA®

Address: 9, Daryaganj, Delhi, 110002, India

275 New North Road Islington Suite 1314 London,
N1 7AA, United Kingdom

ISBN (PBK): 978-93-49887-56-5
ISBN (E-BOOK): 978-93-49887-41-1

Scan the QR code to explore our entire catalogue

www.orangeava.com

Dedicated To

This book was written during a time of profound injustice, as the world witnessed the genocide in Gaza and Palestine. It is dedicated to the people of Gaza and Palestine, who endured unimaginable tragedy, loss, and suffering. May their strength, resilience, and humanity never be forgotten.

In memory of the innocent souls, whose lives were lost in the conflict:
May their spirits find peace.

May this work serve as a small tribute to their resilience. May we all strive for a world grounded in justice, compassion, and human dignity.

And

My wife Ansam, my daughter Rafef, and my son Yunus

About the Author

Muhammad Badawy is a senior DevOps and Platform Engineer with over 12 years of experience at the intersection of development and operations, driving efficiency, scalability, and automation across global cloud environments. Certified as a Kubernetes Administrator (CKA) and AWS Solutions Architect, Muhammad specializes in cloud-native architecture, infrastructure as code, observability, and CI/CD automation.

He has architected and maintained complex systems for leading organizations including ING, Mambu, Mobiquity, and Vodafone, leveraging technologies such as Kubernetes, Helm, Terraform, Azure DevOps, and the ELK stack. Muhammad has a proven track record of accelerating delivery pipelines, optimizing monitoring systems with Prometheus and Grafana, and implementing robust DevSecOps practices.

Currently based in the Netherlands, he is also an active technical writer, contributing expert-level articles to platforms including Medium, Earthly, and StormForge. Beyond engineering, Muhammad is an Arabic Calligrapher with a passion for digital art, and enjoys playing Padel in his free time.

Technical Review Partner

Thinknyx® Technologies is a team of seasoned IT professionals with expertise ranging from software development to the management of IT infrastructure, cloud, automation, container management, web and app development, security, and professional services. Recognized as a trusted brand, Think Nyx® Technologies provides IT consulting, technical and soft skills training as well as talent acquisition and recruitment solutions for organizations across industries.

Mr. Kulbhushan Mayer, Co-Founder of Thinknyx® Technologies, is a certified expert in DevOps, SRE, Cloud, and Containerisation, with over 17 years of experience in the IT industry. His technical expertise spans Public/Private Cloud platforms, Containers, Automation tools, Continuous Integration/ Deployment/Delivery tools, Monitoring and Logging tools, and more. Passionate about knowledge sharing, Mr. Mayer regularly engages with the global tech community through various forums, conferences, webinars, blogs, and LinkedIn. He has also served as a technical reviewer for several books on Automation, DevOps, DevTools, and related technologies.

Acknowledgements

I would like to express my sincere gratitude to everyone who supported the creation of this book.

I am profoundly grateful to the editors and technical reviewers whose insightful guidance and rigorous technical feedback were vital for ensuring clarity and accuracy in every chapter.

A special acknowledgement is extended to the Prometheus open-source community for providing such a powerful and accessible tool. My gratitude also goes to the many engineers and contributors in online forums whose shared expertise enriched this work immensely.

Preface

For cloud-native applications and dynamic infrastructure, observability has become vital for operational excellence. Monitoring systems are expected to deliver real-time insights, proactively detect issues, and scale seamlessly with modern workloads. Prometheus, the open-source monitoring solution developed by SoundCloud and now part of the CNCF, has been considered a standard for metrics collection and alerting in such environments.

This book is a comprehensive, hands-on guide that takes readers from the foundational concepts of monitoring to advanced implementation patterns using Prometheus. It is crafted for DevOps professionals, SREs, developers, and anyone interested in building a robust observability stack.

It offers practical examples, real-world insights, and step-by-step guidance. To reinforce learning, every chapter concludes with Points to Remember and a curated set of Multiple-Choice Questions (MCQs)–ideal for self-assessment, interviews, or preparation for certifications such as the Prometheus Certified Associate (PCA).

This Book Covers:

Chapter 1. Introduction and Key Concepts in Monitoring: This chapter introduces the landscape of modern monitoring, explaining the difference between static and dynamic environments, where Prometheus fits into the DevOps lifecycle, and the stages of metrics monitoring. It also highlights anti-patterns, design patterns, and the relationship between logs and metrics, concluding with a guide on setting up your Prometheus workspace.

Chapter 2. Prometheus Server Architecture and Features: This chapter explores the core architecture and key components of Prometheus, providing a solid foundation for understanding how it collects, stores, and processes metrics. We will learn about the Prometheus server, exporters, instrumentation, the Push Gateway, Service Discovery, and how PromQL enables powerful querying. We will also introduce Alertmanager for basic alert handling. A special focus is given to the Time Series Database (TSDB) - its features, scalability, and handling of high cardinality and dynamic sampling, along with the challenges they may bring.

Chapter 3. Different Types of Prometheus Metrics: In this chapter, we will understand the fundamental metric types: Counters, Gauges, Summaries, and Histograms. This chapter explains when and how to use each type, along with best practices for accurate metric representation.

Chapter 4. Metrics Exporters for Infrastructure Monitoring: In this chapter, we will learn how Prometheus collects data using exporters. This chapter focuses on key exporters such as Node Exporter, BlackBox Exporter, WMI Exporter for Windows, MySQL Exporter, and cAdvisor for container metrics.

Chapter 5. Prometheus Service Discovery Feature: In this chapter, we will explore how Prometheus uses Service Discovery to dynamically find targets in environments such as Kubernetes. The chapter includes a demo setup with prerequisites and implementation of service discovery in action.

Chapter 6. Metrics Labeling and Relabeling: Labels are central to how Prometheus stores and queries data. This chapter discusses the importance of labels, how source and target labels are used, and introduces the relabeling mechanism for refining target configurations.

Chapter 7. Prometheus Query Language PromQL: In this chapter, we will master PromQL with real examples. Topics include aggregation operators, label matchers, grouping (by/without), binary operations, and core functions such as rate, irate, avg_over_time, and count_values. We will also learn which functions work with range vectors.

Chapter 8. Alerts and Alert Receivers: This chapter covers the complete alerting lifecycle in Prometheus. We will earn to define alerts, label and annotate them, and configure Alertmanager for routing, grouping, throttling, and silencing. We will also explore how to integrate with alert receivers like email, Slack, or PagerDuty.

Chapter 9. Advanced Prometheus Techniques: Take your skills to the next level with advanced topics such as securing endpoints with TLS, optimizing storage, writing complex PromQL queries, and integrating with tools like Grafana, Jaeger, and OpenTelemetry for full observability. Additionally, we will learn careful configuration for capacity planning and performance tuning, and also Prometheus automation, which is essential for scaling.

Chapter 10. Prometheus and Real-world Applications: This chapter highlights how Prometheus is applied across real-world architectures, including cloud infrastructure, network monitoring, and DevOps environments. You'll explore how Prometheus supports different teams, the types of metrics it provides, and practical use cases in each domain. We also take a brief look at how companies like SoundCloud and Uber successfully use Prometheus in production.

Chapter 11. Conclusion: Future Steps: Wrap up the journey with a recap of key takeaways, tips for the PCA certification, and guidance on next steps for expanding your observability knowledge and Prometheus practice.

Get a Free eBook

We hope you are enjoying your recently purchased book! Your feedback is incredibly valuable to us, and to all other readers looking for great books.

If you found this book helpful or enjoyable, we would truly appreciate it, if you could take a moment to leave a short review with a 5 star rating on Amazon. It helps us grow, and lets other readers discover our books.

As a thank you, we would love to send you a free digital copy of this book, and a **30%** discount code on your next cart value on our official websites:

www.orangeava.com

www.orangeava.in (For Indian Subcontinent)

☑ **Here's how:**

Leave a review for the book on Amazon.

Take a screenshot of your review, and send an email to **info@orangeava.com** (it can be just the confirmation screen).

Once, we receive your screenshot, we will send you the digital file, within 24 hours.

Thank you so much for your support – it means a lot to us!

Colored Images

Please follow the links or scan the QR codes to download the ***Images*** of the book:

You can find code bundles of our books on our official Github Repository. Go to the following link to and QR code to explore the further:

https://github.com/orgs/ava-orange-education/repositories

Please follow the link to download the Colored Images of the book:
https://rebrand.ly/njlphj4

In case there's an update to the code, it will be updated on the existing GitHub repository.

Errata

We take immense pride in our work at **Orange Education Pvt Ltd,** and follow best practices to ensure the accuracy of our content to provide an indulging reading experience to our subscribers. Our readers are our mirrors, and we use their inputs to reflect and improve upon human errors, if any, that may have occurred during the publishing processes involved. To let us maintain the quality and help us reach out to any readers who might be having difficulties due to any unforeseen errors, please write to us at :

errata@orangeava.com

Your support, suggestions, and feedback are highly appreciated.

DID YOU KNOW

Did you know that Orange Education Pvt Ltd offers eBook versions of every book published, with PDF and ePub files available? You can upgrade to the eBook version at **www.orangeava.com** and as a print book customer, you are entitled to a discount on the eBook copy. Get in touch with us at: **info@orangeava.com** for more details.

At **www.orangeava.com**, you can also read a collection of free technical articles, sign up for a range of free newsletters, and receive exclusive discounts and offers on Print Books and eBooks.

PIRACY

If you come across any illegal copies of our works in any form on the internet, we would be grateful if you would provide us with the location address or website name. Please contact us at **info@orangeava.com** with a link to the material.

ARE YOU INTERESTED IN AUTHORING WITH US?

If there is a topic that you have expertise in, and you are interested in either writing or contributing to a book, please write to us at **business@orangeava.com**. We are on a journey to help developers and tech professionals to gain insights on the present technological advancements and innovations happening across the globe and build a community that believes Knowledge is best acquired by sharing and learning with others. Please reach out to us to learn what our audience demands and how you can be part of this educational reform. We also welcome ideas from tech experts and help them build learning and development content for their domains.

REVIEWS

Please leave a review. Once you have read and used this book, why not leave a review on the site that you purchased it from? Potential readers can then see and use your unbiased opinion to make purchase decisions. We at Orange Education would love to know what you think about our products, and our authors can learn from your feedback. Thank you!

For more information about Orange Education, please visit **www.orangeava.com**.

Table of Contents

CHAPTER 1
Introduction and Key Concepts in Monitoring

Introduction

Prometheus (https://prometheus.io/docs/introduction/overview/) is an open-source monitoring and alerting tool developed for reliability and scalability in modern, dynamic infrastructures. It was originally developed by SoundCloud, which was trying to develop a dynamic, container-based infrastructure and solutions for monitoring at the time. Some of these tools such as Graphite and Nagios did not prove to be adequate for them. They needed something different, a tool that would fit their needs and meet their demands.

Prometheus was initially written by a small crew of ex-Google engineers, and published in 2016. Prometheus is actually inspired by Google's in-house monitoring tool called Borgman. Google utilizes Borgman to oversee its process orchestration tool called Borg.

It is a well-known fact that Borg is the inspiration for Kubernetes. So when you take into consideration the impact that Kubernetes continues to have on the IT world, you can also get a better idea of why Prometheus is such a big deal. Also, Prometheus is the second official CNCF project, following Kubernetes (https://www.cncf.io/announcements/2018/08/09/prometheus-graduates/#:~:text=SAN%20FRANCISCO%2C%20Calif.%2C%20August,its%20second%20project%20to%20graduate%2C).

In this chapter, we will build a base of important key concepts in monitoring before diving into Prometheus. You will learn about the difference between static and dynamic monitoring and where Prometheus lands in the DevOps lifecycle. Also, you will explore the different stages of data monitoring, the relation between logs and metrics, the different mechanisms of collecting data (Pull/Push), and much more.

Structure

In this chapter, we will discuss the following topics:

- Monitoring and Its Importance
- Different Scopes of Monitoring
- Static versus Dynamic Environments
- Prometheus in DevOps Lifecycle
- Stages of Metrics Monitoring
- Anti-patterns in Continuous Monitoring
- Design Patterns in Continuous Monitoring
- Relation between Logs and Metrics
- Pull versus Push
- Setting up Your Workspace

Monitoring and Its Importance

Monitoring is the process of continuously observing and tracking the performance, health, and behavior of systems, applications, or networks. This includes gathering metrics, logs, traces, and any other data about how a system is performing. This data is then analyzed to track performance, detect anomalies, troubleshoot issues, and alert stakeholders of deviations, failures, or potential problems.

The following reasons can be mentioned to highlight the importance of monitoring in modern technologies:

- **Proactive Issue Detection:** Potential problems are detected early before they become critical. This may save time and resources by preventing downtime, data loss, and system failures.
- **Improved Performance:** Monitored performance metrics such as response time, CPU usage, and memory consumption help optimize system performance. Identification of performance bottlenecks enables teams to take corrective action to improve efficiency.
- **Reliability and Availability:** System availability and reliability are maintained through continuous monitoring to reduce downtime. For businesses whose online services rely on it, uninterrupted availability is critical to customer trust and revenue.
- **Resource Optimization:** Monitoring reveals resource usage in terms of CPU, memory, network, and disk usage so organizations can optimize infrastructure

allocation. Identifying underused resources and inefficient processes helps businesses cut costs and improve scalability.

- **Security and Compliance:** Monitoring detects suspicious activity, security breaches and anomalies in real time. It also supports industry standards by ensuring that systems work as expected and comply with regulatory requirements.
- **Data-Driven Decision Making:** Monitoring data is collected and analyzed by businesses for infrastructure upgrades, system optimizations, and future growth plans.

Different Scopes of Monitoring

The scope of monitoring refers to the specific areas or levels of a system that are observed and analyzed. These scopes define what you are monitoring–whether it is the underlying infrastructure, applications, or higher-level business outcomes. Listed in this section are the different scopes of monitoring, along with examples of tools that are commonly used for each of these, as well as how Prometheus fits into the picture.

- **Infrastructure Monitoring:** This scope covers the physical and virtual resources that make up a cloud or on-premise environment, including servers, virtual machines, storage, and networking. It monitors metrics such as CPU usage, memory usage, disk I/O, and network throughput to check that the hardware and virtualization layer are working properly. Tools like Amazon CloudWatch, Nagios, and Zabbix give to the administrators a bird's eye view of system health and alert them of failures or shortages of resources.

  Prometheus fits this scope perfectly as it is designed to collect and store system-level metrics from servers and containers (especially Kubernetes environments).
- **Application Monitoring:** This scope focuses on how applications perform and behave when processing requests, processing data, and engaging users. Key metrics here are response times, error rates, transaction volumes, and application-specific KPIs like API call success rates. Tool sets like New Relic, Dynatrace and AppDynamics dominate this space and provide deep insight into code-level performance and user interactions. Prometheus plays a very important role here, notably for microservices or containerized applications. Developers instrument their code with Prometheus client libraries to expose custom metrics like request latency.
- **Network Monitoring:** Network-level monitoring focuses on connectivity, data flow between cloud components, and between cloud components and end users. For communication purposes, it tracks metrics like latency, packet loss, bandwidth usage, and network errors. Tools such as SolarWinds,

Wireshark, and Cisco Cloud network monitoring are designed for this purpose–identifying bottlenecks or outages in the network layer.

Prometheus could contribute to this scope by collecting network-related metrics from the infrastructure. It may be paired with specialized tools for deeper network analysis, but here it is a supplementary rather than a central tool.

- **Security Monitoring:** This scope covers security monitoring for threats, vulnerabilities, and compliance issues. It analyzes logs, user activity, and network traffic to detect anomalies, unauthorized access, or data breaches. Tools such as Splunk, AWS GuardDuty, and Microsoft Sentinel provide robust security event management and threat detection.

  This is where Prometheus plays a more limited role, as it is designed for performance metrics and not security events. However, it can also monitor security-adjacent metrics like failed login rates or resource abuse via custom exporters or application instrumentation, often feeding data into a larger security monitoring pipeline.

- **End-User Monitoring:** Monitoring at the end-user level records how people experience applications. It monitors page load times, click-through rates, session durations, and error occurrences from the user's perspective. Such tools include Pingdom, New Relic Browser, and Akamai mPulse which often use real user monitoring (RUM) or synthetic testing to simulate interactions. Prometheus does not fit this scope well since it measures server-side rather than client-side data.

Static versus Dynamic Environments

In this section, you will learn the differences between static and dynamic environments and where Prometheus can fit better.

Static environments are characterized by a stable and predictable topology, where the number and configuration of resources remain relatively constant. This typically applies to traditional on-premises deployments with minimal infrastructure changes. On the other hand, dynamic environments are characterized by frequent changes and fluctuations in resource availability. Cloud-based infrastructures, microservices architectures, and DevOps practices often lead to dynamic environments.

Prometheus excels in both static and dynamic environments. For static environments, Prometheus' static configuration method, using YAML files or text files, allows for easy definition of target endpoints and metrics. This static approach works well when the monitored infrastructure remains stable.

In dynamic environments, Prometheus leverages its built-in service discovery capabilities to automatically discover and connect to new endpoints as they come up. This eliminates the need for manual configuration and ensures that Prometheus remains aware of the constantly changing resource landscape.

Prometheus' strengths shine when monitoring dynamic environments. Its ability to handle frequent changes in resource availability makes it ideal for cloud-based deployments, microservices architectures, and DevOps practices. Prometheus can automatically discover new endpoints, add them to monitoring, and generate alerts for any anomalies or performance issues. So, Prometheus is more appropriate for dynamic and modern infrastructure, while other tools such as Zabbix and Nagios are more appropriate for static infrastructure.

Here is a comparison table highlighting the differences between static and dynamic environments and where Prometheus fits better:

Aspect	Static Environment	Dynamic Environment
Topology	Stable and predictable	Frequent changes and fluctuations
Resource Configuration	Constant and relatively unchanging	Variable and constantly evolving
Typical Deployments	Traditional on-premises setups	Cloud-based infrastructures, microservices architectures, DevOps practices
Prometheus Configuration	Uses static configuration methods (YAML or text files)	Utilizes built-in service discovery for automatic endpoint discovery
Manual Effort	Manual configuration required for defining target endpoints	Minimal manual effort due to automatic service discovery
Suitability for Prometheus	Good, as it allows an easy definition of stable infrastructure targets	Excellent, as it handles frequent changes and auto-discovers new endpoints
Monitoring Strengths	Effective for stable infrastructures	Excels in dynamic, modern infrastructures with frequent changes
Comparison to Other Tools	Tools such as Zabbix and Nagios are more suited for static infrastructures	Prometheus is more suited for dynamic and modern infrastructures

***Table 1.1**: Static versus Dynamic Environments*

Prometheus in DevOps Lifecycle

In this section, you will learn about the DevOps lifecycle stages, as well as where Prometheus can land in this cycle. Let us start with the planning and coding stages, which fall under the continuous development aspect of DevOps.

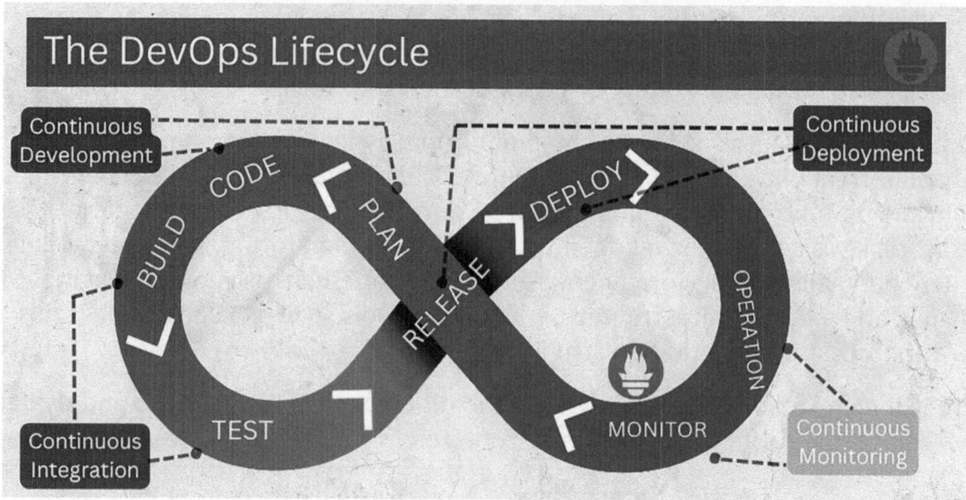

***Figure 1.1**: Prometheus in DevOps Lifecycle*

In the planning stage, objectives are compiled based on customer needs and demands. Once application objectives are defined, the development process begins, constituting the coding section.

After developing code that is aligned with user objectives, the process transitions to the build and testing phase. Attempting to merge code triggers a test, forming the continuous integration aspect of the life cycle, which is essentially the heart of DevOps.

Once the code passes testing and integrates successfully, the process moves to the release stage. This involves releasing and deploying the code into the production environment, constituting continuous deployment in the DevOps life cycle. Configuration management tools like Puppet or Ansible are often employed in the deployment stage to ensure continuity across horizontally scaled environments.

The final two stages are known as continuous monitoring. In the operation stage, the operations team ensures the stability and reliability of production systems, leading to the monitoring stage. This stage is considered the most crucial within the life cycle, allowing for the determination of whether the application code aligns with end-user standards. Here, the health of the system and application performance is assessed, and trends are identified. **Here is the role of Prometheus.**

The monitoring stage provides valuable metrics that contribute to overall performance improvement, including the reduction of support costs, increased productivity, and enhanced system reliability. Analytics and reporting generated in this stage offer clarity for the subsequent planning stage.

To look further into the monitoring aspect, it comprises five stages: data collection, data storage, alerting, visualization, and analytics/reporting. The data collection stage involves servers pulling metrics or agents pushing metrics to the server. Time series data is stored locally or in a cluster environment during the data storage stage. Alerting and visualization, while not in a specific order, address response to events and provide insights into performance trends, respectively. The results of these stages enable the presentation of meaningful analytics and reporting.

Stages of Metrics Monitoring

Effective metrics monitoring involves a well-defined process with distinct stages, each playing a crucial role in gaining actionable insights from data. Here is a breakdown of the 5 essential stages:

1. **Data Collection:** This stage focuses on gathering relevant data from various sources within your system or application. This might include:

    - **System metrics**: CPU usage, memory consumption, network traffic, disk I/O.
    - **Application metrics**: Response times, error rates, transaction volume, custom application-specific metrics.
    - **External data**: Weather data, social media sentiment, customer feedback.

    The chosen data sources and methods should align with your specific monitoring goals and desired insights.

2. **Data Storage:** Collected data needs a reliable and scalable storage solution. Common options include:

    - **Time-series databases**: Optimized for storing and querying time-based data like metrics. Examples: Prometheus, InfluxDB, TimescaleDB.
    - **Relational databases**: Can store both structured and unstructured data, suitable for combining metrics with other relevant information. Examples: MySQL, PostgreSQL.
    - **Cloud storage**: Scalable and flexible storage options such as Amazon S3 or Google Cloud Storage can be used for archiving or long-term data retention.

    Selecting the right storage solution depends on factors such as data volume, frequency of access, and desired retention period.

3. **Alerting:**

    Setting up alerts helps identify and react to critical events promptly. This involves:

    - **Defining thresholds**: Specify acceptable ranges for metrics, triggering alerts when values exceed or fall below those limits.

- **Choosing notification channels**: Email, SMS, Slack, or dedicated alerting services can be used to notify relevant personnel.
- **Fine-tuning alerts**: Minimize false positives by customizing alerts based on specific conditions or patterns.

Effective alerting minimizes downtime and ensures timely intervention during critical situations.

4. **Visualization:** Visualizing data makes it easier to understand trends, identify patterns, and spot anomalies. Common tools include:
   - **Dashboards**: Provide real-time and historical overviews of key metrics, often customizable to user needs.
   - **Charts and graphs**: Line charts, bar charts, heatmaps, and other visualization formats help communicate insights effectively.
   - **Data exploration tools**: Allow users to interactively explore and analyze data through filtering, aggregation, and custom queries.

   Well-designed visualizations make data accessible and actionable for stakeholders across various levels of technical expertise.

5. **Analytics and Reporting:**

   This stage involves using collected data to derive deeper insights and inform decision-making. It encompasses:
   - **Trend analysis**: Identify long-term trends and patterns in metrics to understand system behavior and predict future needs.
   - **Root cause analysis**: Investigate the underlying causes of incidents or performance issues based on historical data and correlations.
   - **Reporting**: Generate reports summarizing key findings, trends, and recommendations for stakeholders.

     Analytics and reporting empower data-driven decision-making, helping optimize system performance, resource allocation, and overall business strategies.

These stages are not strictly linear. Data collection, storage, and visualization often happen simultaneously. The key is to implement a continuous monitoring loop, where insights gained from data analysis inform improvements in data collection and visualization, leading to even more valuable insights.

Anti-patterns in Continuous Monitoring

When integrating new solutions into your tech stack, it is easy to fall into certain pitfalls. Thinking of these as "*anti-patterns*" helps us navigate them more effectively. In this section, we will discuss some common challenges that should be avoided.

- **Reactive Approach**: Only reacting to issues after they occur rather than anticipating and preventing them leads to a reactive, firefighting mode of operation. Adopting a proactive monitoring approach allows teams to identify and mitigate potential issues before they impact users, enhancing system stability and user satisfaction.
- **Ignoring Root Cause Analysis (RCA)**: Focusing only on symptoms and quick fixes without addressing underlying causes can lead to recurring issues, making it difficult to achieve long-term stability. Incorporating Root Cause Analysis (RCA) into the monitoring process helps identify and resolve the root causes of problems, preventing the recurrence of similar issues and improving system reliability.
- **Popularity Does Not Guarantee Success**: Following trends blindly can lead you astray. While it is natural to be drawn to popular tools or solutions used by successful companies, it is crucial to understand their context and assess their fit for your specific needs. Do not be biased by popularity alone. The wide use of Prometheus does not mean that it is the automatic answer for everyone. Take the time to investigate its strengths and weaknesses before making a decision. Remember, the success of a company lies not just in the tools they use, but also in the people and practices behind them.
- **Tool Obsession**: It is tempting to believe that a tool can solve all your problems. However, this mentality breeds "*tool obsession*," where the focus shifts from addressing true needs to simply acquiring the latest and greatest gadgets. Remember, a well-equipped toolbox does not guarantee success. Choose tools based on your specific needs, not just popularity. Do not forget that monitoring involves more than just metrics; consider profiling, tracing, and logging as well. Most importantly, avoid the trap of blaming your tools for shortcomings. Invest in understanding them thoroughly and using them effectively. Tools are only as powerful as the people who wield them.
- **Unnecessary Shortcuts**: Resist the urge for quick fixes and shortcuts. Instead, invest in building a robust and sustainable monitoring environment. This might seem like a bigger upfront investment, but it will save you time and effort in the long run. Do not waste time toiling away on repetitive tasks; learn new tool features and leverage automation whenever possible. Automate tedious tasks like adding targets manually, especially in large-scale environments with hundreds or even thousands of endpoints. Embrace service discovery to ensure scalability and efficiency. Remember, your time is valuable, and automation is your friend, not your foe.
- **Alert Overload**: Generating too many alerts can overwhelm the team, causing significant issues to be overlooked due to the sheer volume of notifications.

This anti-pattern can be mitigated by implementing alert prioritization, grouping related alerts, and using threshold tuning to minimize noise, thus ensuring that the team focuses on the most critical alerts and maintains high efficiency.

By understanding and avoiding these common issues, you can make informed decisions when choosing and implementing solutions for your tech stack.

Design Patterns in Continuous Monitoring

Effective monitoring goes beyond simply implementing tools. Design patterns in continuous monitoring refer to best practices and structured approaches for effectively and efficiently monitoring systems, applications, and services. To truly optimize performance and gain valuable insights, consider these powerful design patterns:

- **Service Discovery and Dynamic Configuration**: Automatically discovers services and dynamically updates monitoring configurations. This is particularly useful in highly dynamic environments like microservices and container orchestration platforms. Tools such as Consul, etcd, and Kubernetes support this pattern.
- **Master Modularity with Composability**: Move beyond monolithic setups. Instead, utilize a modular design built from specialized tools, each excelling in its specific function. This approach offers flexibility and adaptability, allowing you to easily swap or upgrade individual components while maintaining system integrity. Example: Consider Prometheus for collecting metrics, Grafana for visualization, and `Alertmanager` for notifications, instead of relying on a single, all-encompassing tool.
- **Black Box Monitoring**: White Box Monitoring is about observing the system from an external viewpoint, focusing on the end-user experience. This pattern is useful for synthetic monitoring, external health checks, and uptime monitoring, and tools such as Pingdom and New Relic Synthetics are commonly used for this purpose.
- **White Box Monitoring**: White Box Monitoring involves detailed, internal monitoring of systems, applications, and services. It is used for monitoring application performance, system metrics, and internal health indicators. Prominent tools for white box monitoring include Prometheus, Grafana, and Datadog.
- **User-Centric Monitoring**: Remember that your monitoring system exists to serve your users. Prioritize metrics directly impacting their experience. A high CPU spike on a node may seem alarming, but if it does not affect user-facing performance, it might not be a critical issue. Align your monitoring strategy with user needs and expectations for true value.

- **Invest in Proven Solutions**: Building in-house tools might seem cost-effective at first, but consider the hidden costs. Established tools benefit from dedicated development teams, extensive testing, and large user communities. This translates to broader functionality, better documentation, and ongoing bug fixes–advantages your in-house solution might struggle to match. Evaluate existing tools critically before committing to the development burden. Remember, buying might save you valuable time and resources in the long run.
- **Distributed Tracing**: Tracking requests across various services and components in a distributed system. It is especially useful in microservices architectures for understanding service dependencies and identifying performance bottlenecks. Jaeger, Zipkin, and OpenTelemetry are tools that enable distributed tracing.
- **Event-Driven Monitoring**: Refers to monitoring systems that respond to specific events or triggers. This pattern is useful for real-time alerting and response, particularly in serverless architectures. Tools such as AWS CloudWatch Events and Azure Event Grid are designed for event-driven monitoring.

These design patterns offer a roadmap to optimize your monitoring system and gain crucial insights for improved performance, user experience, and overall IT effectiveness. Remember, these are not rigid rules, but guiding principles to adapt and refine based on your specific needs and context.

Relation Between Logs and Metrics

While metrics and logs are both essential tools in the monitoring toolbox, they serve distinct purposes and offer complementary insights.

Figure 1.2: *Relation Between Logs and Metrics*

Metrics: The Big Picture, Without the Details

Think of metrics as the quantitative snapshots of your system's health. They track aggregations over time, like average response times or error rates. Metrics lack context, but their strength lies in providing a wide-angle view, helping you to quickly identify potential issues. Imagine them as alarms, alerting you to anomalies in the system's heartbeat.

Logs: Deep Dives for Context

When metrics point you towards a subsystem causing trouble, logs become your investigative tool. They offer detailed, contextual information about specific events–individual user requests, error messages, or system interactions. Like detective work, logs help you understand the "*why*" behind the "*what*" identified by metrics. Think of them as magnifying glasses allowing you to zoom in and examine the specifics.

Metrics and logs are not competitors, but rather partners in crime-solving. Metrics provide the initial clues, guiding you toward potential trouble spots. Logs then offer the backstory, allowing you to pinpoint the root cause and understand the specific events at play.

Pull versus Push

The debate between push and pull data monitoring techniques often sparks heated discussions, each claiming superiority over the other. However, deciding between push and pull ultimately depends on your specific needs and environment.

***Figure 1.3**: Pull versus Push Techniques*

The push method operates like a text message notification. An agent actively collects metrics from monitored sources and sends them to a central server. This approach excels in real-time updates and scenarios where continuous internet access is limited. Additionally, horizontal scaling is easy with push–you simply deploy more servers with the same configuration file. Sharing setups with new team members is also effortless, and achieving high availability is as simple as running multiple servers pulling data from the same targets. However, this method can introduce complexity in managing and configuring the agents and may pose security concerns, as data needs to be securely transmitted from multiple sources to the central server.

On the other hand, pull monitoring resembles checking social media posts. The monitored source actively broadcasts metrics on an endpoint, and the server periodically pulls data from this location. This technique shines in lightweight environments in which the server needs explicit knowledge of the place where data can be found. However, this method can be less scalable due to the increased load on the server, especially in large-scale environments with numerous monitored entities. Additionally, data collected via the pull technique might not be as up-to-date as in a push system, depending on the polling frequency, and it can generate significant network traffic due to continuous polling.

Choosing the right fit between push and pull can be determined based on several factors: your network environment, the need for real-time updates, scalability requirements, and desired complexity. Evaluate your specific context carefully to make an informed decision.

How it Works in Prometheus

Prometheus primarily uses a **pull technique** for collecting metrics. It periodically queries the configured endpoints (called targets) to fetch their metrics. These targets expose their metrics via HTTP endpoints, usually in the form of /metrics. Then, Prometheus scrapes these endpoints at regular intervals, which are defined in the configuration.

The pull-based approach offers several advantages with Prometheus. It provides a centralized configuration, allowing the server to control when and how often to scrape each target, thereby offering a single point of management. This method is also flexible and dynamic, easily adapting to changes in the environment such as adding or removing targets, with service discovery mechanisms automating much of this process. Additionally, Prometheus excels in error detection, as the server can readily identify when a target is down or unreachable.

While Prometheus uses the pull model, it also provides a way to support push-based metrics collection through the **`Pushgateway`**, which will be discussed in the next chapter.

Here is a comparison to highlight the main differences between pull and push techniques in monitoring:

Feature	Pull Technique	Push Technique
Definition	The monitoring server queries the monitored entities to retrieve metrics or logs.	Monitored agents send metrics or logs to the monitoring server.
Control	Centralized control; the monitoring server dictates when and how data is collected.	Decentralized control; each agent determines when to send data.
Configuration	Managed from the server side, providing a single point of management.	Requires configuration on each monitored agent.
Scalability	Can be less scalable due to increased load on the monitoring server.	Generally, more scalable as data collection is distributed.
Real-time Data	Data collection may have higher latency depending on the polling interval.	Can provide near real-time updates as data is pushed immediately.
Network Efficiency	May generate significant network traffic due to periodic polling.	Typically, more efficient, as only necessary data is pushed.
Error Detection	Easier to detect and handle errors or non-responsive agents.	More challenging to detect issues unless the server tracks expected data intervals.
Environment Adaptability	Adapts to changes dynamically, such as adding/removing targets, especially with service discovery.	Requires manual reconfiguration or automation to adapt to changes in monitored entities.
Data Loss	Data is less likely to be lost as the server actively retrieves it.	Potential for data loss if the monitoring server is down or unreachable.
Security	Centralized security management; fewer points of vulnerability.	Requires securing multiple data transmission points from agents to servers.
Implementation Examples	Prometheus (primary method), Nagios, Zabbix.	StatsD, collectd, Telegraf, Prometheus (`Pushgateway`)

Table 1.2: *Comparison Between Pull and Push Techniques*

Setting Up Your Workspace

In all the demos that will be provided across the book, you need to have a Prometheus installed in your machine. Running Prometheus in a Docker container is an excellent way to streamline its deployment, ensuring that the setup is consistent and easily manageable. Here is a step-by-step guide for installing Prometheus using Docker.

Prerequisites: Before you start, ensure you have **Docker** installed on your machine. You can download and install Docker from this installation link: https://docs.docker.com/engine/install/

Step-by-Step Installation

1. **Pull the Prometheus Docker Image**

   The first step is to pull the Prometheus Docker image from the Docker Hub repository. You can do this by running the following command in your terminal:

   ```
   docker pull prom/Prometheus
   ```

2. **Create a Prometheus Configuration File**

   Prometheus uses a configuration file (**`prometheus.yml`**) to define its behavior, including what to monitor and how to scrape metrics. Create a directory to store this configuration file and navigate to it:

   ```
   mkdir prometheus
   cd prometheus
   ```

   Create a **`prometheus.yml`** file with the following basic configuration:

   ```
   global:
     scrape_interval: 15s  # Set the scrape interval to every 15
   seconds. Default is every 1 minute.

   scrape_configs:
     - job_name: 'prometheus'
       static_configs:
         - targets: ['localhost:9090']
   ```

   This configuration tells Prometheus to scrape its own metrics every 15 seconds and expose them through the default port "**`9090`**" at localhost.

3. **Run Prometheus Container**

   Now, you can run the Prometheus container using the following Docker command. This command will map the host's port 9090 to the container's port 9090 and mount the configuration file:

   ```
   docker run  -d  --name prometheus  -p 9090:9090 -v $(pwd)/pro-
   metheus.yml:/etc/prometheus/prometheus.yml  prom/prometheus
   ```

   - **`-d`** runs the container in detached mode.
   - **`--name`** prometheus names the container "**`prometheus`**".
   - **`-p 9090:9090`** maps port 9090 of the host to port 9090 of the container.

- **`-v $(pwd)/prometheus.yml:/etc/prometheus/prometheus.yml`** mounts the local **`prometheus.yml`** file to the container.

4. **Verify the Installation**

   To ensure Prometheus is running correctly, open your web browser and navigate to **http://localhost:9090**. You should see the Prometheus web interface.

   You can also verify the container status by running:

   ```
   docker ps
   ```

   This command lists all running containers. Look for the Prometheus container in the output.

Conclusion

You are now familiar with all the basic concepts associated with monitoring. You know the theory behind Prometheus and where it comes from. You know where Prometheus can fit better and in which environment. You are also aware of some patterns to follow for efficient and continuous monitoring, and other patterns to avoid, and you have a basic background about pull and push techniques.

In the next chapter, we will dive into Prometheus architecture, exploring each component and its features.

Points to Remember

- Prometheus fits better in dynamic environments compared to static environments.
- Prometheus lands in the Continuous Monitoring stage of the DevOps lifecycle.
- Metrics monitoring starts with Data Collection, moving to Data Storage to Visualization and Alerting, and ends with Analytics and Reporting.
- There are patterns to follow and others to avoid for effective continuous monitoring.
- Metrics and logs complement each other. Metrics are for a high-level view, and logs for deeper investigation.
- Prometheus uses a pull technique, which means it scrapes metrics from exposed endpoints at the application side.

Multiple Choice Questions

1. What is the default port of the Prometheus server?
    a. 8080
    b. 9090
    c. 8081
    d. 9091
2. Which technique does Prometheus use?
    a. Pull
    b. Push
    c. Pull for the server and push for Prometheus Gateway
    d. None
3. In which environment can Prometheus fit better?
    a. Static
    b. Dynamic
    c. Both
    d. None
4. What is the first stage of Metrics monitoring?
    a. Data Storage
    b. Data Collection
    c. Alerting
    d. Visualization
5. Black-Box monitoring is one of the design patterns in Continuous monitoring.
    a. True
    b. False
6. The reactive approach is one of the anti-patterns in Continuous monitoring.
    a. True
    b. False

Answers

1. b
2. c
3. b
4. b
5. a
6. a

CHAPTER 2

Prometheus Server Architecture and Features

Introduction

Prometheus is a static binary written in Golang and designed for powerful observability. It utilizes a pull method for data collection, scraping metrics from targets that have exporters generating HTTP endpoints. For short-lived batch jobs such as cron jobs, Prometheus employs the Push Gateway. This allows such jobs to send metrics to the Push Gateway, which Prometheus then scrapes. Additionally, Prometheus can dynamically discover targets through tools such as Consul or cAdvisor, which are essential in dynamic environments.

In this chapter, you will learn about every component of Prometheus architecture and the features introduced by every component. You will also explore Time Series Database (TSDB) and learn how scraped metrics are stored in specific disks customized for fast reads and writes.

Structure

In this chapter, we will discuss the following topics:

- Prometheus Architecture Components
    - Prometheus Server
    - Exporters and Instrumentation
    - Push Gateway
    - Service Discovery
    - PromQL and Data Querying
    - Alert Manager

- Prometheus Server Features
- Time Series Database in Prometheus (TSDB)
    - Features of Time Series Databases
    - Advanced Capabilities of Time Series Databases

Prometheus Architecture Components

Prometheus's flexible architecture makes it highly scalable and suitable for monitoring dynamic environments like cloud-native and containerized systems.

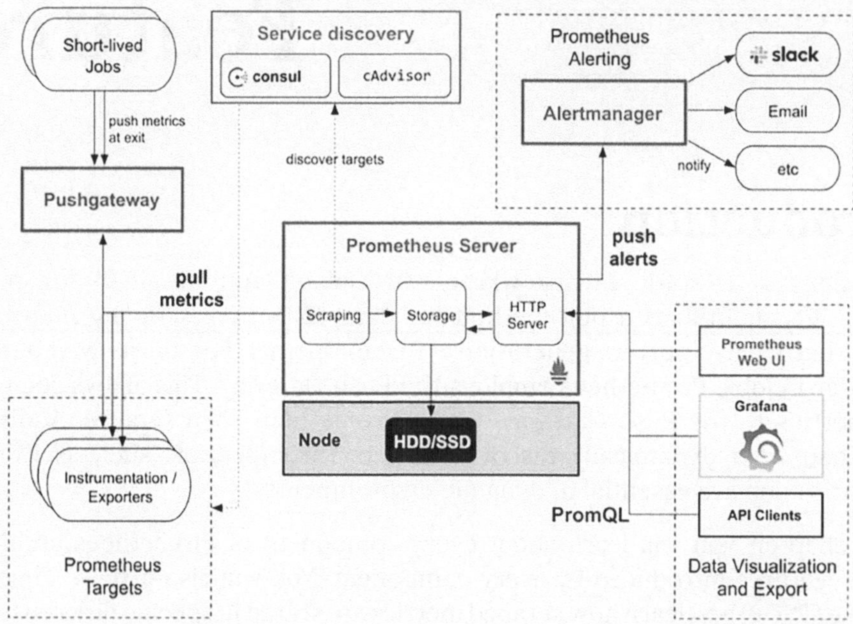

Figure 2.1*: Prometheus Architecture Components*

In this section, we will walk through the key components of Prometheus architecture, exploring their characteristics and the roles they play in the Prometheus ecosystem.

Prometheus Server

The Prometheus server is the core component of the architecture. It is responsible for scraping and storing time-series data from various targets. The server is a single static binary written in Golang, which simplifies deployment and ensures efficient performance. It uses **a pull-based model**, actively scraping metrics from instrumented services and applications that expose HTTP endpoints. This design choice offers greater control over the data collection process and facilitates easier debugging and testing.

Now let us explore how Prometheus stores and manages data:

- **Time Series Data Model**: Metrics data in Prometheus is stored as time series, which are identified by a unique metric name and a set of key-value pairs called labels. These labels allow for multidimensional data organization and powerful querying capabilities. Each time series consists of a sequence of timestamped values, making it easy to track changes over time.
- **Local Storage**: Prometheus stores its data locally on disk in a custom format optimized for time-series data. The local storage engine uses a write-ahead log (WAL) to ensure data durability. The WAL records incoming data before it is written to the main database files, providing a mechanism to recover data in case of a crash.
- **Block Storage**: Prometheus organizes stored data into blocks. Each block typically covers a fixed time range (usually two hours). Within each block, data is stored in chunks, and metadata about the time series is kept separately. This block-based structure allows for efficient data management, querying, and compaction.
- **Compression**: To optimize storage usage and performance, Prometheus periodically compacts smaller blocks into larger ones and applies various compression techniques to reduce the size of stored data. Compaction helps in managing storage efficiently and improves query performance by reducing the number of blocks that need to be accessed.
- **Retention Policies**: Users can configure retention policies to manage the lifecycle of stored metrics data. By setting a retention period, users can control how long data is kept before it is deleted, balancing the need for historical data with storage cost considerations.
- **Remote Storage Integrations**: While Prometheus primarily uses local storage, it also supports remote storage integrations. This allows users to offload older or less frequently accessed data to external systems, ensuring long-term storage and high availability. Remote storage options include systems such as Thanos, Cortex, and others that provide scalable and durable storage backends.

Exporters and Instrumentation

To gather metrics, Prometheus relies on exporters and direct instrumentation. Exporters are tools that collect metrics from third-party systems (such as databases, hardware devices, or other software) and expose them in a format Prometheus can scrape. For instance, the Node Exporter collects hardware and OS-level metrics from Linux nodes. Direct instrumentation involves embedding Prometheus client libraries in application code to expose custom metrics, providing detailed insights into application behavior.

More details about exporters will be provided in *Chapter 4, Metrics Exporters for Infrastructure Monitoring.*

Push Gateway

For short-lived batch jobs and ephemeral tasks that might not be around for the next scrape cycle, Prometheus uses the Push Gateway. Batch jobs push their metrics to the Push Gateway, which holds the metrics until Prometheus scrapes them.

Use Cases for Push Gateway

- **Batch Jobs:** Batch jobs, such as cron jobs or data processing tasks, may start and finish in a very short time frame, making them unsuitable for direct scraping by Prometheus. By pushing metrics to the Push Gateway at the end of their execution, these jobs ensure that their performance data is captured.
- **Ephemeral Jobs:** In a dynamic environment, jobs that are created and destroyed quickly (for example, serverless functions or transient containers) benefit from the Push Gateway. These jobs can push their metrics as soon as they are completed.
- **Standalone Scripts:** Standalone scripts or utilities that do not run continuously can also use the Push Gateway to report their metrics. This is particularly useful for scripts that are triggered by external events and do not have a long-running lifecycle.

The Push Gateway adds flexibility to the Prometheus monitoring ecosystem, However, it is important to consider that using the Push Gateway introduces some complexity:

- **Transient State:** Metrics in the Push Gateway are inherently transient and may be lost if the Push Gateway is restarted. Therefore, it is not suitable for metrics that need to be persisted long-term.
- **Metric Lifecycle Management:** Administrators need to manage the lifecycle of metrics within the Push Gateway to ensure that old or irrelevant metrics are cleaned up appropriately.
- **Alerting and Deduplication:** Care must be taken when defining alerts for metrics pushed to the Push Gateway to avoid false positives or duplicate alerts, especially if multiple instances of the same job push similar metrics.

Service Discovery

In dynamic environments, such as those involving microservices or cloud-native architectures, static configuration of scrape targets is impractical. Prometheus supports service discovery mechanisms to automatically discover and monitor new services as they come online. It ensures that the monitoring configuration stays up-to-date without manual intervention.

Prometheus supports various service discovery tools, listed as under:

- **Kubernetes**: Prometheus can discover services running in a Kubernetes cluster by querying the Kubernetes API. It can automatically detect new pods, services, and endpoints, making it ideal for monitoring containerized applications.
- **Consul**: Consul is a service mesh solution that provides service discovery and configuration. Prometheus can integrate with Consul to discover services registered in the Consul catalog.
- **DNS**: Prometheus can use DNS-based service discovery to resolve hostnames into IP addresses. This is useful for environments where DNS is used for service registration and discovery.
- **EC2**: Prometheus can discover instances in Amazon EC2 by querying the AWS API. It can automatically detect new instances and their associated metadata.
- **Azure**: Similar to EC2, Prometheus can discover virtual machines and services in Microsoft Azure by querying the Azure API.
- **DigitalOcean**: Prometheus can discover Droplets (virtual machines) in DigitalOcean by querying the DigitalOcean API.
- **Custom SD Integrations**: Prometheus supports a file-based service discovery mechanism, where a file containing a list of targets is periodically read and updated. This allows for custom integrations with other service discovery systems.

More details about Service Discovery features will be covered in *Chapter* 5, *Prometheus Service Discovery Feature.*

Time Series Database (TSDB)

The Time Series Database (TSDB) is a crucial part of Prometheus, responsible for storing all the scraped metrics. Prometheus's TSDB is designed for high performance and efficiency. It stores data in a custom format on disk, optimized for fast writes and reads. The TSDB handles features such as data compression and compaction, ensuring that storage remains efficient and scalable. Data retention policies can be configured to manage the lifecycle of stored metrics, balancing between storage costs and the need for historical data.

More details about TSDB will be provided in a later section of this chapter.

PromQL and Data Querying

PromQL (Prometheus Query Language) is the query language used by Prometheus to retrieve and manipulate time series data. It is designed specifically for working with time series data, providing powerful capabilities for aggregation, filtering, and mathematical operations. Users can run queries via the Prometheus web interface, enabling them to explore and visualize metrics. For more advanced and customizable dashboards, Prometheus integrates seamlessly with Grafana, a popular open-source visualization tool.

We will dive into PromQL capabilities in *Chapter 7, Prometheus Query Language PromQL.*

Alertmanager

Alerting in Prometheus is managed by the Alertmanager. Alerts are defined in the Prometheus server based on specific conditions in the metrics data. When these conditions are met, the Alertmanager handles the routing of alerts to various notification channels, such as email, Slack, PagerDuty, and others. The Alertmanager also provides features like grouping, and silencing of alerts, ensuring that notifications are actionable and not overwhelming. It can be scaled horizontally and configured to communicate with other Alertmanager instances for high availability.

More details about Alerts and Alert Receivers will be provided in *Chapter 8, Alerts and Alert Receivers.*

Prometheus Server Features

In this section, we will highlight the main features of Prometheus, including a pull-based metrics collection model, high ingestion rates, support for application instrumentation, and more.

- **Time-Series Database:** Prometheus is fundamentally a monitoring solution with a built-in time series database. This database is optimized for storing time series data, which is crucial for tracking the state of systems over time and analyzing trends.
- **Single Static Binary:** The Prometheus server is implemented as a single static binary built in Golang. This design simplifies deployment and management, as it does not require complex dependencies or installations. The static nature of the binary ensures that the server is easy to distribute and run across various environments.
- **Pull-Based Metrics Collection:** Prometheus collects metrics using a pull-based model. It scrapes metrics from instrumented targets by sending HTTP

requests to their endpoints. This method provides better control over the timing and frequency of data collection, making it easier to handle monitoring configurations and updates.

- **Metrics from Various Sources:** Prometheus can pull metrics from a wide range of sources, including network devices, hosts, services, and applications. This versatility allows it to monitor the health and performance of virtually any component within an IT infrastructure.
- **Application Instrumentation:** Prometheus supports application instrumentation with numerous client libraries for different programming languages, such as Golang, Python, JavaScript, and Ruby. These libraries allow developers to instrument their applications easily, providing detailed and custom metrics that reflect the internal state and performance of the applications.
- **High Ingestion Rate:** The Prometheus server is designed to handle a high volume of metrics, capable of ingesting millions of metric data points per second. This high ingestion rate makes it suitable for large-scale environments with numerous monitored targets generating significant amounts of data.
- **Workaround Solutions for Pull-Based Model:** Although Prometheus primarily uses a pull-based model, it provides solutions for scenarios where a push-based approach is necessary. For instance, the Push Gateway component allows short-lived jobs to push their metrics to a gateway, which Prometheus then scrapes. This flexibility ensures that Prometheus can handle various use cases and environments effectively.
- **Multi-Dimensional Data Model:** Prometheus uses a multi-dimensional data model, where metrics are stored as time series identified by a metric name and a set of key-value pairs (labels). This model allows for powerful and flexible querying and aggregation of metrics based on different dimensions.
- **PromQL for Querying:** Prometheus Query Language (PromQL) is a specialized query language designed for time series data. It provides robust querying capabilities, enabling users to perform complex operations on the collected metrics, such as filtering, aggregation, and mathematical calculations.
- **Service Discovery:** Prometheus supports various service discovery mechanisms to automatically discover and monitor new targets. It integrates with tools such as Kubernetes, Consul, and DNS, ensuring that the monitoring setup remains up-to-date as the environment changes dynamically.
- **Alerting and Integration with Alertmanager:** Prometheus includes built-in alerting capabilities. Users can define alerting rules to trigger alerts based on specific conditions in the metrics data. These alerts can be managed and routed using the Alertmanager, which supports deduplication, and groups, and sends notifications to various channels such as email, Slack, and PagerDuty.

- **Local Storage and Remote Storage Options:** Prometheus stores its time series data locally on disk, which ensures fast read and write operations. Additionally, it can be configured to use remote storage solutions for long-term storage or more extensive scalability needs.
- **Visualization:** While Prometheus includes a basic built-in web interface for querying and visualizing metrics, it is often paired with Grafana for more advanced and customizable dashboards. Grafana provides extensive support for Prometheus as a data source, allowing users to create detailed visualizations and dashboards.

Time Series Database in Prometheus (TSDB)

A database optimized for storing and retrieving time-stamped or time series data.

***Figure** 2.2: Time Series Database*

A Time Series Database (TSDB) is a specialized type of database designed for efficiently storing, querying, and managing time-stamped data. This kind of data is crucial in a variety of fields, such as finance, health monitoring, and IT systems. By organizing data points in a sequence indexed by time, TSDBs can handle the high volume and velocity of data generated by modern applications, enabling fast and cost-effective storage and retrieval of time series data. Prominent examples of TSDBs include Prometheus, which offers unique capabilities to meet the needs of effective observability.

Time series data comprises measurements or events tracked, monitored, and aggregated over a period. For instance, monitoring CPU usage over time involves recording the CPU's state at consistent intervals, creating a sequence of data points that reflect changes over time. Unlike traditional databases, which might store static records, a TSDB is optimized for this dynamic, ever-changing data landscape.

Each time series record in a TSDB typically includes a time-stamp and a value, forming pairs such as:

- **`@ timestamp1 → value1`**
- **`@ timestamp2 → value2`**

This simple structure allows for efficient data compression and quick access, which are critical for performance monitoring and alerting systems.

Features of Time Series Databases

Time Series Databases (TSDBs) come with key features that make them very powerful for managing and analyzing time-stamped data. The following are some of the key features of TSDB:

- **Efficient Storage and Retrieval:** TSDBs are designed to handle large volumes of time series data efficiently. They employ various compression techniques to store data compactly, which is essential given the potentially massive scale of time series data generated by modern applications. This efficiency allows for both cost-effective storage and rapid retrieval of data, enabling real-time analysis and monitoring.
- **Scalability:** One of the primary features of TSDBs is their ability to scale horizontally. As the volume of data grows, TSDBs can distribute the load across multiple nodes, ensuring consistent performance without significant latency increases. This scalability is crucial for applications that generate high-frequency data, such as IoT devices or high-traffic web applications.
- **High-Resolution Data Storage:** TSDBs support the storage of high-resolution data, allowing for very granular insights. This capability is vital for detecting short-lived anomalies or patterns that might be missed with less frequent sampling. For example, monitoring system performance at 15-second intervals can provide a more detailed view of the system's health than minute-by-minute data.

Advanced Capabilities of Time Series Databases

In this section, you will explore two advanced topics in observability, high cardinality, and dynamic sampling, and how they affect the behavior of monitoring systems.

High Cardinality

High cardinality refers to the number of unique values that a particular attribute or dimension in a dataset can take. In the context of time series data, high cardinality often involves numerous unique identifiers, such as user IDs, IP addresses, transaction IDs, or device IDs. These unique identifiers can generate many distinct time series, making data management and querying more complex.

Importance of High Cardinality

High cardinality is crucial for detailed and granular analysis. For example, in a web application, monitoring user activities at the individual level can help identify specific user behaviors, detect anomalies, and personalize user experiences. High cardinality allows for tracking and analyzing these activities with precision.

Examples of High Cardinality

- **User Activity Monitoring**: Consider a scenario where an e-commerce platform wants to monitor the browsing and purchasing behavior of its users. Each user has a unique user ID, and each action (such as a page view, click, or purchase) generates a time series entry. With potentially millions of users, the system needs to handle high cardinality efficiently to provide real-time insights and analytics.
- **IoT Device Monitoring**: In an industrial IoT setup, each device (for example, sensors, machines) has a unique identifier. Monitoring each device's performance metrics, such as temperature, vibration, and uptime, results in a high cardinality dataset. Effective handling of this data allows for predictive maintenance and optimization of industrial processes.
- **Financial Transactions**: In financial markets, each transaction can be uniquely identified by transaction IDs, customer IDs, and asset IDs. Tracking these transactions over time helps in fraud detection, compliance monitoring, and performance analysis of different financial instruments.

Dynamic Sampling

Dynamic sampling is a technique used to manage and optimize data storage and query performance in time series databases. Instead of storing every single data point, dynamic sampling involves selectively storing high-value or high-signal data points while sampling lower-value or low-signal data points at a lower rate. This ensures that critical information is preserved for analysis without overwhelming the storage system.

Importance of Dynamic Sampling

Dynamic sampling is essential for balancing the trade-offs between data resolution, storage costs, and query performance. By focusing on the most relevant data, organizations can maintain efficient data systems and still derive meaningful insights from their time series data.

Examples of Dynamic Sampling

- **Error Tracking in Software Systems**: In a large-scale software system, error logs might be generated continuously. Storing every error log can quickly become unmanageable. Instead, dynamic sampling can be used to store all critical errors (high-signal data) while sampling non-critical errors (low-signal data) at a lower rate. This ensures that important issues are captured and analyzed without excessive storage overhead.

  In this scenario, **high-signal data** includes critical errors such as application crashes or security breaches, which are stored in detail, capturing every instance to allow thorough investigation and timely response. On the other hand, **low-signal data** consists of non-critical warnings or routine log entries that are sampled at a lower rate. For example, instead of storing every instance of a non-critical warning, the system might store every tenth instance or summarize the occurrences over a period of time. This approach ensures that essential information is retained for analysis while reducing the storage and processing load of less significant data.

- **Network Traffic Monitoring**: For a network administrator, monitoring traffic patterns is crucial for identifying potential security threats and performance issues. High-traffic periods might generate an overwhelming amount of data. Dynamic sampling can be applied to ensure that anomalous traffic patterns (high-signal data) are captured in detail, while routine traffic (low-signal data) is sampled less frequently.

  High-signal data, such as unusual spikes in traffic, signs of a potential DDoS attack, or significant performance drops, are captured in detail. This ensures that critical events are recorded comprehensively, enabling quick identification and response to potential issues. On the other hand, **low-signal data**, such as normal, steady traffic, is sampled less frequently. Instead of logging every packet during normal operation, the system might aggregate data over longer intervals or sample fewer packets, reducing storage requirements and focusing resources on more important data points.

- **IoT Sensor Data**: In a smart home system, various sensors continuously report data such as temperature, humidity, and motion. While constant monitoring is useful, storing every single data point from every sensor can be impractical. Dynamic sampling allows for detailed storage of significant changes or anomalies (for example, sudden temperature spikes) while sampling routine, stable readings at a lower rate.

  High-signal data, such as sudden temperature spikes, indications of smoke or gas, or significant motion detected while the house is supposed to be empty, are stored in detail. This ensures that critical and potentially dangerous events are captured comprehensively, allowing for timely interventions and detailed analysis. On the other hand, **low-signal data**, like routine temperature readings or humidity levels that do not vary significantly, are sampled at lower rates. For instance, instead of logging every temperature reading every second, the system might record the average temperature every minute. This approach optimizes storage and processing resources while still maintaining enough data for effective monitoring and analysis.

Combining High Cardinality and Dynamic Sampling

Combining high cardinality and dynamic sampling allows for the efficient handling of complex and voluminous time series data. Here are the ways in which this is achieved:

- **Enhanced Anomaly Detection**: High cardinality enables the identification of anomalies at a granular level, such as detecting unusual user behavior on an e-commerce site. Dynamic sampling ensures that significant anomalies are captured in detail while routine data is sampled, optimizing storage and performance.
- **Optimized Resource Utilization**: By focusing on high-signal data and reducing the storage of low-signal data, dynamic sampling helps manage high-cardinality datasets without overwhelming the database infrastructure. This leads to optimized resource utilization and cost savings.
- **Detailed Insights with Manageable Data**: Organizations can achieve detailed insights into their operations without the need for excessive data storage. High cardinality provides the depth of data needed for comprehensive analysis, while dynamic sampling ensures that the most relevant information is retained.

While high cardinality and dynamic sampling are powerful techniques for managing time series data, they come with notable drawbacks.

Drawbacks of High Cardinality

- **Increased Storage Requirements:** High cardinality datasets can significantly increase storage requirements. Each unique identifier (such as user IDs, device IDs, and more) generates a distinct time series, leading to a substantial volume of data that needs to be stored. This can quickly overwhelm storage capacities, especially in large-scale systems with millions of unique identifiers.
- **Performance Degradation:** As the number of unique time series increases, the performance of data retrieval and querying operations can degrade. High cardinality can strain the database's indexing and querying mechanisms, leading to slower response times and increased latency in data retrieval. This

can be particularly problematic in real-time monitoring systems where timely access to data is crucial.

- **Complexity in Data Management:** Managing high cardinality data can be complex. It requires more sophisticated indexing, partitioning, and sharding strategies to maintain efficient access and retrieval. Additionally, ensuring data consistency and managing metadata for numerous unique identifiers can add to the administrative overhead.
- **Resource Intensive:** Handling high cardinality datasets often requires more computational resources, including memory and CPU. This can lead to higher operational costs and may necessitate investment in more powerful hardware or cloud resources to maintain acceptable performance levels.

Drawbacks of Dynamic Sampling

- **Loss of Granularity:** Dynamic sampling inherently involves sacrificing some level of data granularity. While it helps in managing storage and processing resources, it also means that some detailed information is lost. For low-signal data, this might be acceptable, but if sampling parameters are not well-tuned, important patterns or anomalies could be missed.
- **Potential for Missed Anomalies:** In scenarios where low-signal data can occasionally exhibit important variations, dynamic sampling might miss these anomalies. If significant events occur within the periods of reduced sampling, they may go undetected, potentially leading to incomplete or inaccurate monitoring and analysis.
- **Complex Configuration:** Implementing dynamic sampling requires careful configuration to balance between data retention and granularity. Determining appropriate sampling rates and thresholds for high-signal and low-signal data can be complex and may require continuous adjustment based on the changing nature of the monitored systems.
- **Impact on Long-Term Analysis:** Dynamic sampling can affect long-term trend analysis and historical data comparison. As older data gets downsampled, the loss of detailed information can impact the accuracy of long-term analyses and forecasting. This can be particularly challenging in applications that rely on detailed historical data for predictive modeling and trend analysis.

Conclusion

The core of Prometheus architecture is the Prometheus Server, which ingests, processes, and stores metric data in a highly efficient Time Series Database (TSDB). The TSDB provides features like efficient storage and retrieval, scalability, and high-resolution data storage, making it well-suited for monitoring complex systems. Complementing this is the Push Gateway, which facilitates the handling of ephemeral job metrics, and the Alert Manager, which enables intelligent alerting and notification mechanisms. The system's Service Discovery capabilities allow seamless integration with dynamic infrastructure, while PromQL, Prometheus' powerful query language, empowers users to extract meaningful insights from collected data. Together, these components ensure that Prometheus remains adaptable, scalable, and capable of meeting diverse monitoring needs.

The advanced capabilities of time series databases, such as high cardinality and dynamic sampling, enhance Prometheus' ability to process large volumes of data and provide fine-grained analysis. However, these strengths come with challenges, including increased resource consumption and potential complexity in data management. Despite these drawbacks, Prometheus strikes a balance, offering users a flexible, reliable platform for modern observability needs. Its modular design, extensibility through exporters and instrumentation, and community support make it an indispensable tool for developers and operators alike, ensuring proactive monitoring and optimized system performance. In the next chapter, you will explore different types of Prometheus metrics including counters, gauges, histograms, and summaries.

Multiple Choice Questions

1. Which of the following is the core component of Prometheus architecture responsible for data ingestion and querying?
    a. Push Gateway
    b. Prometheus Server
    c. Alert Manager
    d. Service Discovery
2. What is the primary role of the Push Gateway in Prometheus?
    a. To store long-term data
    b. To collect and send metrics from short-lived jobs
    c. To manage alerts and notifications
    d. To discover new services automatically
3. For which purpose is PromQL in Prometheus used?
    a. Alerting
    b. Service discovery
    c. Querying time-series data
    d. Exporting metrics

4. Which feature of the Time Series Database (TSDB) in Prometheus allows it to store data at varying levels of granularity?
   a. High cardinality
   b. Dynamic sampling
   c. Scalability
   d. Efficient storage and retrieval
5. What is the function of Service Discovery in Prometheus?
   a. To alert operators about system failures
   b. To find and track targets dynamically in a changing environment
   c. To store high-resolution data
   d. To manage short-lived job metrics
6. What drawback is commonly associated with high cardinality in time series databases?
   a. Difficulty in querying data
   b. Reduced data resolution
   c. Increased resource consumption
   d. Loss of data accuracy
7. Which component in Prometheus is responsible for managing notifications and alert thresholds?
   a. Prometheus Server
   b. Alert Manager
   c. Push Gateway
   d. TSDB
8. What type of data storage does the Prometheus Time Series Database focus on?
   a. High-performance relational database storage
   b. Distributed file system storage
   c. High-resolution time-series data storage
   d. Object-based storage

9. How does Prometheus handle dynamic infrastructure changes?
    a. Using manual configurations
    b. Through Service Discovery
    c. By utilizing static targets
    d. With help from third-party applications
10. Which of the following is NOT an advanced capability of time series databases in Prometheus?
    a. High cardinality
    b. Dynamic sampling
    c. Relational data joins
    d. Fine-grained data retrieval

Answers

1. b
2. b
3. c
4. b
5. b
6. c
7. b
8. c
9. b
10. c

Chapter 3

Different Types of Prometheus Metrics

Introduction

Metrics are the measures used to track and assess the performance, health, and behavior of a system. In the context of Prometheus and monitoring systems, metrics provide critical data points that represent various aspects of system performance.

Metrics have several **key characteristics** that make them essential for performance monitoring and analysis. They are **inherently quantitative**, providing numerical values that represent specific performance indicators such as CPU usage, memory consumption, or request counts. This quantitative nature allows for precise measurement and comparison. **Metrics are recorded over time**, forming time series data, which is crucial for trend analysis, anomaly detection, and historical comparisons. Additionally, metrics often **include contextual information** in the form of labels or tags, which offer further details about the metric, such as its source, the type of operation being performed, or other relevant contexts. This additional information helps in understanding and interpreting the metrics more effectively, facilitating better decision-making and diagnostics.

Metrics are fundamental to effective monitoring as they provide critical insights into the performance, capacity, and reliability of systems. They play a vital role in **performance monitoring**, allowing organizations to track application and infrastructure metrics such as CPU usage and response times, which can highlight performance bottlenecks. Metrics also support **capacity planning** by enabling the analysis of historical data to forecast future resource requirements and scale infrastructure accordingly. Through **anomaly detection**, continuous monitoring helps identify unusual patterns or spikes, signaling potential issues or attacks. Furthermore, metrics underpin **proactive alerting systems**, which notify administrators of problems before they affect users, ensuring system reliability and uptime.

In addition to preventive capabilities, metrics are invaluable for diagnosing and improving systems. They aid in **root cause analysis** by providing data to trace issues back to their origins, such as correlating spikes in error rates with recent deployments or traffic changes. Metrics also drive optimization efforts by offering insights into system behavior under varying conditions, thus enabling more efficient and reliable operations. This data-driven approach empowers organizations to maintain robust, high-performing systems while continuously improving their infrastructure.

In Prometheus, metrics are categorized into four main types: counters, gauges, histograms, and summaries. Each type serves different purposes and provides unique insights into system performance.

This chapter will explore these four types of Prometheus metrics: counters, gauges, histograms, and summaries. You will learn their definitions, characteristics, and use cases, providing practical examples to illustrate how each type can be effectively utilized for monitoring and alerting. By the end of this chapter, you will have a comprehensive understanding of these metrics and how to utilize them to gain valuable insights into your system's performance.

Structure

In this chapter, we will discuss the following topics:

- Counters in Prometheus Metrics
  - Use Cases for Counters
  - Examples of Counters
  - Best Practices for Using Counters
  - Advanced Usage of Counters
- Gauges in Prometheus Metrics
  - Use Cases for Gauges
  - Examples of Gauges
  - Best Practices for Using Gauges
  - Advanced Usage of Gauges
- Histograms in Prometheus Metrics
  - Use Cases for Histograms
  - Examples of Histograms
  - Best Practices for Using Histograms
  - Advanced Usage of Histograms
- Summaries in Prometheus Metrics
  - Use Cases for Summaries
  - Examples of Summaries

- Best Practices for Using Summaries
- Advanced Usage of Summaries

Counters in Prometheus Metrics

A counter in Prometheus is a type of metric that represents a single cumulative value that can only increase over time or be reset to zero. Counters are used to track the occurrence of specific events or the total amount of something over time.

Key characteristics of counters:

- **Monotonically Increasing**: Counters only increase; they never decrease. This property makes them ideal for tracking things that accumulate over time, such as requests served or errors encountered.
- **Reset to Zero**: Counters can be reset to zero, usually upon system restart or when an application restarts. Prometheus is designed to handle these resets gracefully.

As shown in *Figure* 3.1, the graph of the `**go_gc_duration_seconds_count**` counter demonstrates these key characteristics. This specific metric tracks the count of garbage collection (GC) cycles that have occurred in a Go application. As you see, the value consistently increases over time, reflecting the accumulating count of garbage collection cycles. This increasing pattern is shown by the upward steps in the graph. If the counter resets, Prometheus will still show the correct rate of increase both before and after the reset.

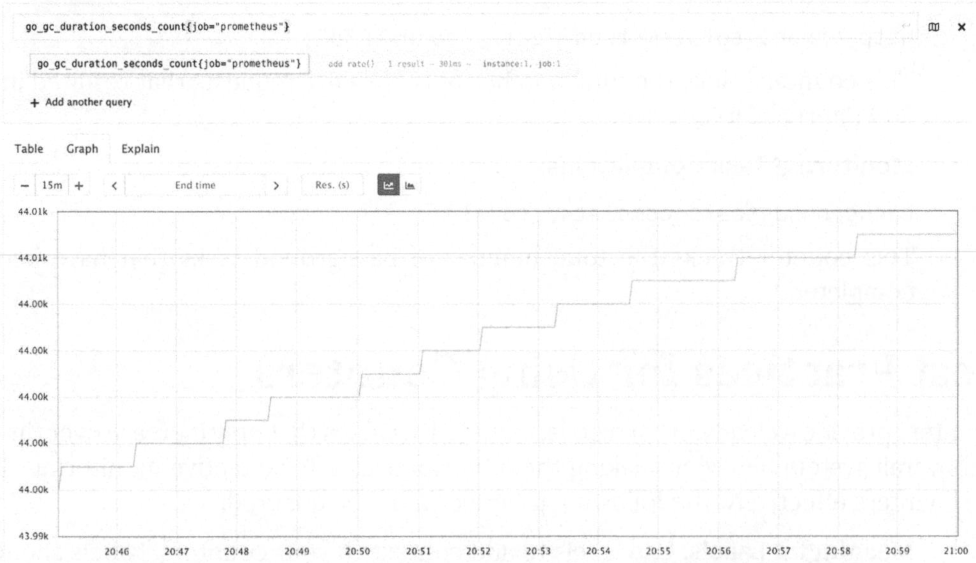

Figure 3.1: *go_gc_duration_seconds_count metric filtered by Prometheus job*

Use Cases of Counters

Counters are particularly useful for tracking metrics that represent counts of events or total amounts of resources consumed. Here are some common use cases:

- **Number of HTTP Requests**: Track the total number of HTTP requests received by a web server.
- **Error Counts**: Track the number of errors that have occurred, such as failed login attempts or system errors.
- **Task Completions**: Monitor the number of tasks that have been completed in a background job processing system.
- **Bytes Transferred**: Measure the total amount of data sent or received over a network connection.

Examples of Counters

The following are examples of counter metrics and what they do:

- **Tracking HTTP Requests:**

  ```
  http_requests_total{method="post", code="200"}
  ```

  This counter tracks the total number of HTTP POST requests that have resulted in a 200 status code. The **`{method="post", code="200"}`** part is a set of labels providing additional context to the metric.

- **Counting Errors:**

  ```
  http_errors_total{method="get", code="500"}
  ```

  This counter tracks the total number of HTTP GET requests that resulted in a 500 internal server error.

- **Monitoring Task Completions**:

  ```
  background_tasks_completed_total
  ```

  This counter tracks the total number of background tasks that have been completed.

Best Practices for Using Counters

Counters provide a clear view of trends, cumulative values that only increase over time, and overall system behavior, making them indispensable for effective monitoring. To use counters effectively, the following practices must be ensured:

- **Meaningful Labels**: Use labels to add context to your counters. Labels should be chosen carefully to provide meaningful insights without leading to high cardinality, which can negatively impact performance.

```
http_requests_total{method="post", endpoint="/api/v1/
users", status="200"}
```

- **Balance High Cardinality**: Be mindful of the number of unique label combinations. High cardinality can lead to performance issues and increased memory usage.

```
# Bad example (potentially high cardinality)
user_login_attempts_total{user_id="12345"}

# Better example (lower cardinality)
user_login_attempts_total{status="success"}
user_login_attempts_total{status="failure"}
```

The first query is a bad example of cardinality because it involves a unique identifier (**`user_id`**) that can result in an extremely large number of unique time series when used at scale. By using a label like status instead of a unique identifier like `` `user_id` ``, you significantly reduce the number of unique time series. For example, if you have only a few possible values for status (for example, "**`success`**", "**`failure`**"), the number of time series remains small and manageable.

- **Reset Handling**: Design your monitoring to handle counter resets gracefully. Prometheus can handle resets by recognizing jumps to lower values and treating them as new series.

```
process_start_time_seconds
```

- **Use Counters for Additive Values**: Counters should only be used for metrics that naturally increase over time. For values that can both increase and decrease, use gauges instead.

```
# Good counter example
disk_io_operations_total{device="sda", type="read"}

# Bad counter example (use a gauge instead)
disk_free_bytes{device="sda"}
```

Advanced Usage of Counters

Prometheus provides several functions that can be applied to counters in queries to derive meaningful insights:

- **`rate()` Function**: Calculates the per-second average rate of increase of a counter over a specified time range.

```
rate(http_requests_total[5m])
```

- **`increase()` Function**: Calculates the total increase of a counter over a specified time range.

```
increase(http_requests_total[1h])
```

- **`irate()` Function**: Similar to **`rate()`**, but calculates the per-second rate of increase based on the two most recent data points. Useful for high-resolution queries.

  ```
  irate(http_requests_total[1m])
  ```

- **`resets()` Function**: Calculates the number of times a counter has reset over a specified time range.

  ```
  resets(http_requests_total[1d])
  ```

Gauges in Prometheus Metrics

A gauge is a type of metric in Prometheus that represents a single numerical value that can freely go up and down. Unlike counters, which can only increase, gauges are used to measure values that can both increase and decrease over time.

Key characteristics of gauges:

- **Arbitrary Values**: Gauges can hold any value and are not restricted to increasing only.
- **Snapshot of State**: They provide a snapshot of the current state of a system, making them ideal for representing values that can fluctuate.
- **Dynamic Nature**: Gauges can be used to measure both instantaneous and continuously changing values.

As shown below, the graph of the **`go_memstats_heap_alloc_bytes`** gauge demonstrates these key characteristics. The values fluctuate over time, reflecting the dynamic nature of heap memory allocation in the Go application. This gauge captures the current state of memory allocation, providing a real-time snapshot of how memory usage varies.

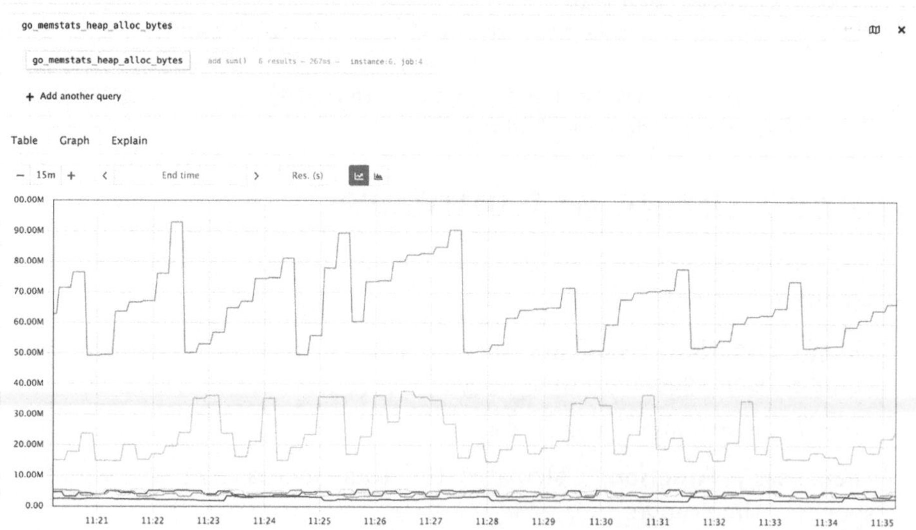

Figure 3.2: *go_memstats_heap_alloc_bytes gauge metric*

Use Cases for Gauges

Gauges are useful for tracking metrics that represent a current state or value, such as resource usage, capacity, or instantaneous measurements. Here are some common use cases:

- **Memory Usage**: Track the amount of memory currently being used by an application or system.
- **CPU Utilization**: Monitor the current CPU usage as a percentage.
- **Concurrent Requests**: Measure the number of ongoing requests being processed by a server.
- **Temperature Readings**: Record the current temperature from a sensor.
- **Queue Length**: Track the number of items currently in a processing queue.

Examples of Gauges

The below are examples of gauges metrics and what they do:

- **Memory Usage**:

  ```
  memory_usage_bytes{instance="localhost:9090"}
  ```

  This gauge tracks the current memory usage in bytes on an instance running on localhost at port 9090.

- **CPU Utilization**:

  ```
  cpu_utilization_percentage{instance="localhost:9090"}
  ```

  This gauge represents the current CPU utilization as a percentage of the same instance.

- **Concurrent Requests**:

  ```
  concurrent_requests{service="webserver"}
  ```

  This gauge measures the number of concurrent requests being handled by a web server.

- **Temperature Reading**:

  ```
  temperature_celsius{sensor="sensor1"}
  ```

  This gauge records the current temperature in Celsius from a sensor named "sensor1".

- **Queue Length**:

  ```
  queue_length{queue="task_queue"}
  ```

  This gauge tracks the number of items currently in a task queue.

Best Practices for Using Gauges

To effectively use gauges, it's important to go beyond simply placing them on a dashboard or interface. Consider the following best practices to ensure your gauges communicate the right information clearly:

- **Meaningful Labels**: Use labels to provide context to your gauges. Labels should be used to differentiate different sources or aspects of the metric.

  ```
  memory_usage_bytes{instance="localhost:9090", container="app_
  container"}
  ```

- **Avoid High Cardinality**: Similar to counters, be cautious with the number of unique label combinations. High cardinality can lead to performance issues.

  ```
  # Bad example (potentially high cardinality)
  queue_length{user_id="12345"}
  # Better example (lower cardinality)
  queue_length{priority="high"}
  queue_length{priority="low"}
  ```

- **Clear Definitions**: Ensure gauges are well-defined and consistently used across your monitoring setup. Define what each gauge measures and ensure consistency.

  ```
  cpu_temperature_celsius{instance="localhost:9090"}
  ```

- **Reset Awareness**: Be aware that gauges can reset, especially in environments where components restart frequently. Design your monitoring to handle such scenarios.

- **Use Gauges for Current States**: Gauges are ideal for metrics that represent the current state or value, as opposed to counters that represent cumulative counts.

  ```
  # Good gauge example
  free_disk_space_bytes{disk="/dev/sda1"}

  # Bad gauge example (use a counter instead)
  total_requests{endpoint="/api/v1/resource"}
  ```

Advanced Usage of Gauges

Prometheus provides several functions that can be applied to gauges in queries to derive meaningful insights:

- **`avg_over_time()` Function**: Calculates the average value of a gauge over a specified time range.

  ```
  avg_over_time(memory_usage_bytes[5m])
  ```

- **`min_over_time()` Function**: Finds the minimum value of a gauge over a specified time range.
  ```
  min_over_time(cpu_utilization_percentage[1h])
  ```
- **`max_over_time()` Function**: Finds the maximum value of a gauge over a specified time range.
  ```
  max_over_time(temperature_celsius[1d])
  ```
- **`deriv()` Function**: Calculates the derivative of a gauge (the rate of change) over a specified time range.
  ```
  deriv(queue_length[5m])
  ```
- **`predict_linear()` Function**: Predicts the future value of a gauge based on linear regression.
  ```
  predict_linear(free_disk_space_bytes[1h], 3600)
  ```

Histograms in Prometheus Metrics

A histogram in Prometheus is a type of metric that collects and counts observations, such as the time that requests take or the sizes of responses, and sorts them into different groups called buckets. This helps in understanding how the values are spread out, which is especially useful for analyzing factors such as response times or data sizes.

Key characteristics of histograms:

- **Buckets**: Histograms group observations into predefined buckets. Each bucket represents a range of values, and the histogram tracks the count of observations falling into each bucket.
- **Cumulative Counts**: The count in each bucket includes all observations that fall into that bucket and any preceding buckets. This cumulative count allows for efficient computation of percentiles.
- **Sum and Count**: In addition to bucket counts, histograms also track the total sum of all observed values and the total count of observations, facilitating the calculation of averages and other statistics.

As shown below, the graph demonstrates the distribution of HTTP request durations over time. Each step represents a bucket of request durations that are less than or equal to a specified threshold, in this case, 1 second.

`` `prometheus_http_request_duration_seconds_bucket{handler="/graph", instance="prometheus:9090", job="prometheus", le="1"}` `` retrieves the cumulative count of requests handled by the /graph endpoint, with durations less than or equal to 1 second. This helps visualize the frequency of such requests and understand the performance of the monitored endpoint.

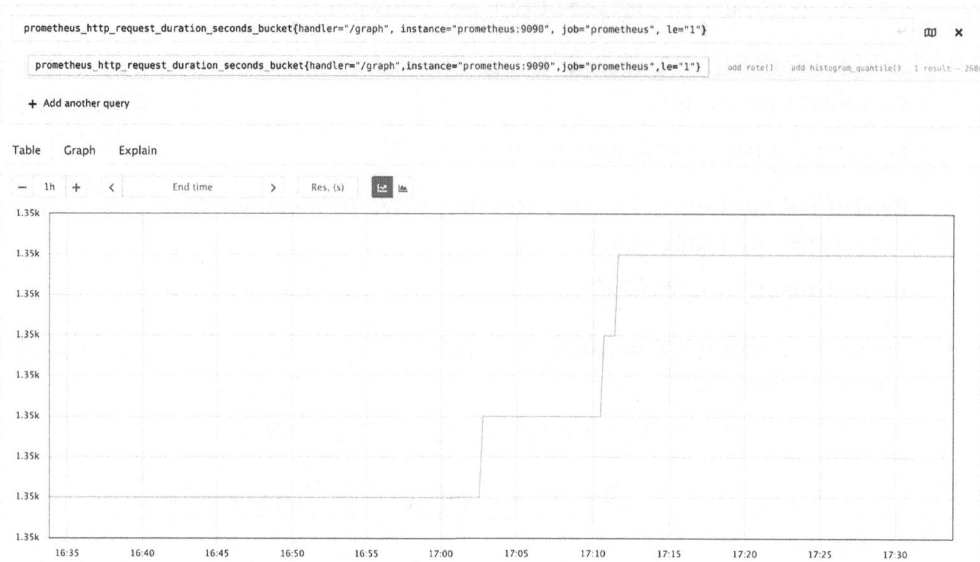

Figure 3.3: *prometheus_http_request_duration_seconds_bucket Histogram Metric*

Use Cases for Histograms

Histograms help understand the distribution of values, especially when dealing with latency, durations, or sizes. Common use cases include:

- **Request Latency**: Measure the distribution of request durations to identify performance bottlenecks.
- **Response Sizes**: Analyze the distribution of response sizes to understand data transfer patterns.
- **Processing Times**: Track the time taken for tasks or operations to complete, providing insights into system efficiency.
- **Resource Usage**: Monitor distributions of resource usage, such as CPU or memory consumption over time.

Examples of Histograms

The following are sample of histogram metrics and what they do:

Request Latency:

```
http_request_duration_seconds_bucket{le="0.1"}
http_request_duration_seconds_bucket{le="1"}
http_request_duration_seconds_bucket{le="+Inf"}
```

```
http_request_duration_seconds_sum
http_request_duration_seconds_count
```

This histogram tracks HTTP request durations. Buckets represent ranges of request durations (for example, up to 0.1 seconds, up to 1 seconds, and more). The `+Inf` bucket includes all requests, ensuring all observations are counted.

Response Sizes:

```
http_response_size_bytes_bucket{le="500"}
http_response_size_bytes_bucket{le="10000"}
http_response_size_bytes_bucket{le="+Inf"}
http_response_size_bytes_sum
http_response_size_bytes_count
```

This histogram tracks the size of HTTP responses, with buckets representing different size ranges.

Best Practices for Using Histograms

Histogram metrics are invaluable for measuring the distribution of values, such as response times or request sizes, across predefined buckets. To effectively leverage histograms, ensure the following practices:

- **Define Appropriate Buckets**: Choose bucket boundaries that make sense for the metric you are measuring. For example, when measuring request latency, you might choose buckets such as 0.1s, 0.2s, 0.5s, 1s, and so on.

  ```
  http_request_duration_seconds_bucket{le="0.1"}
  ```

- **Balance Granularity and Performance**: More buckets provide finer granularity but can increase storage and processing overhead. Find a balance that meets your needs without overwhelming your system.

  ```
  http_request_duration_seconds_bucket{le="0.01"}
  ```

- **Label Consistency**: Use consistent labels to differentiate between similar metrics. Ensure that labels provide meaningful context.

  ```
  http_request_duration_seconds_bucket{method="GET", path="/api/v1/
  users", le="0.1"}
  ```

- **Monitor Bucket Usage**: Regularly review the distribution of observations across buckets to ensure they are appropriately defined. Adjust buckets if necessary to capture the most meaningful data.

  ```
  http_request_duration_seconds_bucket{le="0.1"}
  ```

- **Consider Metric Cardinality**: Be cautious of high cardinality, from too many or very detailed labels, as it can affect performance.

```
# Avoid excessive label combinations
http_request_duration_seconds_bucket{user_id="12345", le="0.1"}
```

Advanced Usage of Histograms

Before going through the advanced usage of Histograms, let us review the quantiles concept. Quantiles are statistical measures that divide a set of observations into intervals with equal probabilities or represent specific points in the data distribution. They help in understanding the distribution of the data, identifying central tendencies, and observing variability and outliers.

Types of Quantiles

- **Median (50th Percentile):** The median is the value separating the higher half from the lower half of a data set. It is the 50th percentile, meaning that 50% of the data points are below this value, and 50% are above it.
- **Percentiles**
    - Percentiles indicate the relative standing of a value within a dataset. The 90th percentile, for instance, is the value below which 90% of the data points lie.
    - **Example**: In a test scored by 100 students, if a student scores higher than 90 students, their score is at the 90th percentile.

Prometheus offers various functions for histograms that help extract useful insights:

- **`histogram_quantile()` Function**: Calculates quantiles (for example, median, 90th percentile) from histogram buckets.

```
histogram_quantile(0.5, sum(rate(http_request_duration_seconds_
bucket[5m])) by (le))
```

- **`rate()` Function**: Calculates the per-second average rate of increase of the time series in each bucket.

```
rate(http_request_duration_seconds_bucket[5m])
```

- **`sum()` and `count()` Functions**: Aggregate the sum and count across different dimensions.

```
sum(rate(http_request_duration_seconds_sum[5m])) by (job)
count(rate(http_request_duration_seconds_count[5m])) by (job)
```

- **`increase()` Function**: Calculates the total increase of bucket counts over a specified time range.

```
increase(http_request_duration_seconds_bucket[1h])
```

Summaries in Prometheus Metrics

A summary in Prometheus is a type of metric that captures the distribution of observed values over a sliding time window and calculates configurable quantiles (for example, median, 90th percentile). Summaries are useful for measuring the total count, sum, and specific quantiles of a set of observations, providing a comprehensive view of the distribution and trends.

Key characteristics of summaries:

- **Quantile Calculation**: Summaries calculate quantiles directly on the client side, allowing for real-time quantile estimation.
- **Sliding Time Window**: Observations are kept over a configurable sliding time window, meaning older observations are eventually discarded.
- **Total Count and Sum**: Summaries track the total count of observations and their sum, enabling the calculation of averages and other statistics.
- **Precision**: Quantiles can be configured to have different error tolerances, offering flexibility in balancing precision and resource consumption.

The below summary query **`prometheus_engine_query_duration_seconds{job="prometheus", quantile="0.5", slice="queue_time"}`** provides the median queue time for queries processed by Prometheus. This means it tells you the middle value of the queue times for all the queries: half of the queries had a queue time less than or equal to this value, and the other half had a queue time greater than this value.

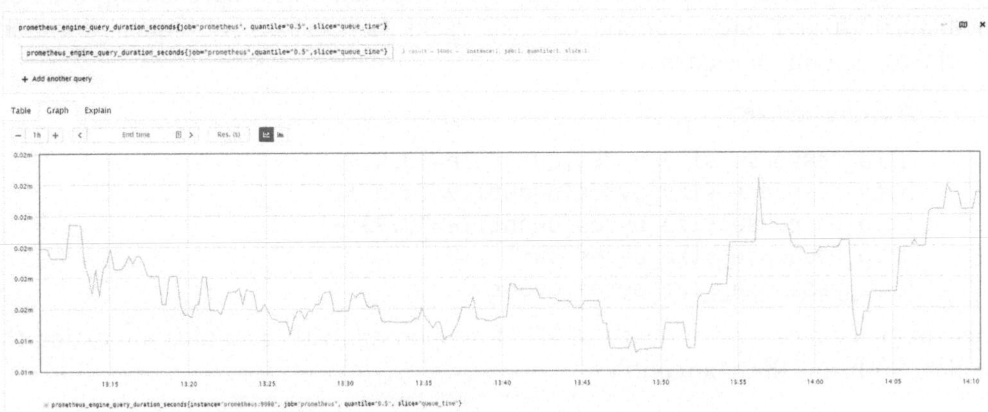

Figure 3.4: *prometheus_engine_query_duration_seconds Summary Metric filtered by job, quantile and slice*

Use Cases for Summaries

Summaries are particularly useful when you need to compute quantiles of a distribution and track trends over time. Common use cases include:

- **Request Latency Quantiles**: Measure specific quantiles of request durations to understand the typical and outlier response times.
- **Response Size Quantiles**: Track quantiles of response sizes to analyze data transfer patterns.
- **Event Processing Times**: Monitor quantiles of processing times for tasks or events to identify performance characteristics.
- **Custom Metrics**: Use for any custom metric where quantile information is valuable, such as user interaction times or system load.

Examples of Summaries

The below are sample of summary metrics and what they do:

- **Request Latency:**

```
http_request_duration_seconds{quantile="0.5"}
http_request_duration_seconds{quantile="0.9"}
http_request_duration_seconds{quantile="0.99"}
http_request_duration_seconds_sum
http_request_duration_seconds_count
```

This summary tracks HTTP request durations, with quantiles representing the 50th (median), 90th, and 99th percentiles. It also tracks the total sum of request durations and the total count of requests.

- **Response Size:**

```
http_response_size_bytes{quantile="0.5"}
http_response_size_bytes{quantile="0.9"}
http_response_size_bytes{quantile="0.99"}
http_response_size_bytes_sum
http_response_size_bytes_count
```

This summary measures the size of HTTP responses, with quantiles indicating the median, 90th, and 99th percentiles.

Best Practices for Using Summaries

To use summaries effectively, ensure considering the following practices:

- **Configure Quantiles Thoughtfully**: Select quantiles that provide meaningful insights into your metric. Common choices are the 50th (median), 90th, and 99th percentiles.

```
http_request_duration_seconds{quantile="0.5"}
```

- **Understand Precision and Resource Usage**: Quantiles in summaries are approximate and come with a trade-off between accuracy and resource consumption. Choose error tolerances that fit your use case.

```
http_request_duration_seconds{quantile="0.99", error="0.001"}
```

- **Avoid High Cardinality**: Be cautious with the number of unique label combinations. High cardinality can impact performance and storage.

```
# Bad example (potentially high cardinality)
http_request_duration_seconds{user_id="12345", quantile="0.5"}

# Better example (lower cardinality)
http_request_duration_seconds{endpoint="/api/v1/resource",
quantile="0.5"}
```

- **Use Summaries for Client-Side Quantiles**: Since quantiles are calculated on the client side, summaries are ideal for use cases where you need immediate quantile estimates without relying on server-side aggregation.

```
http_request_duration_seconds{quantile="0.9"}
```

- **Combine with Other Metrics**: Use summaries in conjunction with other types of metrics, such as counters and gauges, to gain a holistic view of system performance.

```
http_request_duration_seconds_sum
http_request_duration_seconds_count
```

Advanced Usage of Summaries

Prometheus provides functions that can be used in queries to extract and analyze summary data:

- **`quantile()` Function**: Although summaries already calculate quantiles on the client side, the quantile() function can be used to extract quantile information from other data series.

```
quantile(0.99, http_request_duration_seconds)
```

- **`rate()` Function**: Calculates the per-second rate of increase of the count or sum of observations in a summary.

```
rate(http_request_duration_seconds_sum[5m])
rate(http_request_duration_seconds_count[5m])
```

- **`sum()` and `count()` Functions**: Aggregate the sum and count of observations across different dimensions.

  ```
  sum(rate(http_request_duration_seconds_sum[5m])) by (job)
  count(rate(http_request_duration_seconds_count[5m])) by (job)
  ```

- **`increase()` Function**: Calculates the total increase of the sum or count of observations over a specified time range.

  ```
  increase(http_request_duration_seconds_sum[1h])
  increase(http_request_duration_seconds_count[1h])
  ```

Summaries are a powerful and flexible type of metric in Prometheus, designed to capture and analyze the distribution of observed values with quantile estimations. They are particularly useful for understanding latency, size distributions, and other performance characteristics in real-time. By using summaries effectively and following best practices, you can gain deep insights into your system's behavior, helping you to optimize performance, identify bottlenecks, and ensure efficient operation.

Conclusion

In this chapter, we have explored the diverse types of metrics offered by Prometheus, each serving a distinct purpose in monitoring and analyzing system performance and behavior. By understanding the unique characteristics and applications of counters, gauges, histograms, and summaries, you can harness the full potential of Prometheus to gain valuable insights into your systems and applications.

Each type of metric serves distinct and vital roles in monitoring and analyzing system metrics. Counters track cumulative counts of discrete events, such as HTTP requests or errors, with their monotonically increasing nature, ensuring a reliable record of activity over time. In contrast, gauges capture values that can fluctuate, such as memory usage, CPU utilization, or concurrent request counts, making them indispensable for monitoring dynamic, real-time states and resource levels.

For more detailed analysis, histograms group observations into buckets, revealing the frequency and distribution of metrics such as request durations or response sizes. This facilitates comprehensive performance evaluations and trend identification. Lastly, summaries provide an aggregated snapshot of observed values, including counts, sums, and quantiles, enabling precise data distribution analysis and real-time quantile calculations, particularly useful for metrics such as latency and size. Together, these metric types offer a holistic view of system behavior and performance.

By using these metrics effectively, you can build a robust monitoring and alerting system that not only tracks the health and performance of your infrastructure but also provides actionable insights to optimize and maintain your services. The strategic use of Prometheus metrics will enable you to detect and diagnose issues swiftly, improve resource utilization, and ensure that your applications and systems meet the desired performance and reliability standards.

In summary, Prometheus metrics empower you to monitor your systems comprehensively and proactively, fostering a deeper understanding of your infrastructure and enhancing your ability to maintain a high level of service quality.

In the next chapter, you will explore different metrics exporters and how they are used to scrape metrics from different sources, and then pulled by the Prometheus server.

Points to Remember

- Metrics are quantitative data points used to measure system performance, health, and behavior.
- Metrics in monitoring are time-series data, collected and recorded over time for trend analysis and anomaly detection.
- Labels or tags add context to metrics, helping with filtering, aggregation, and better understanding.
- Metrics are critical for:
    - Performance monitoring
    - Capacity planning
    - Anomaly detection
    - Proactive alerting
    - Root cause analysis
    - System optimization
- Prometheus categorizes metrics into four types:
    - **Counters**: Monotonically increasing values (for example, total requests)
    - **Gauges:** Values that can go up or down (for example, temperature, memory usage)
    - **Histograms:** Measure observations over configurable buckets (for example, request duration)
    - **Summaries:** Similar to histograms, but calculate configurable quantiles
- Each metric type serves specific monitoring needs and has unique characteristics and best practices.
- Understanding the proper use of each metric type is essential for accurate observability and system improvement.

Multiple Choice Questions

1. Which of the following is NOT a characteristic of metrics?
   a. They are qualitative
   b. They are time-series data
   c. They include contextual information
   d. They are used for anomaly detection
2. In Prometheus, which metric type is suitable for measuring a value that only increases over time?
   a. Gauge
   b. Counter
   c. Histogram
   d. Summary
3. What type of Prometheus metric should you use to track memory usage that fluctuates up and down?
   a. Counter
   b. Histogram
   c. Gauge
   d. Summary
4. What is the primary purpose of using labels in metrics?
   a. To encrypt metric data
   b. To provide visualizations
   c. To give additional context to the metric
   d. To compress data
5. Which of the following metrics can provide quantile information such as the 95th percentile response time?
   a. Gauge
   b. Counter
   c. Summary
   d. Counter with labels

Answers

1. a
2. b
3. c
4. c
5. c

CHAPTER 4
Metrics Exporters for Infrastructure Monitoring

Introduction

Prometheus metrics exporters are a critical part of any Prometheus-based monitoring setup. They provide the necessary bridge between Prometheus and the wide variety of systems, services, and applications that need to be monitored. By collecting and exposing metrics in a format that Prometheus can understand, exporters ensure that you can maintain a comprehensive and cohesive monitoring environment tailored to your specific needs.

This chapter will explore four types of Prometheus metric exporters: Node Exporter, BlackBox Exporter, WMI Windows Exporter, MySQL Exporter, and cAdvisor Exporter. You will learn their functionalities, characteristics, and use cases, with practical examples to illustrate how each type can be effectively utilized for collecting metrics for different systems. By the end of this chapter, you will have a comprehensive understanding of how metrics are collected from Linux, Windows machines, Databases, and containers.

Structure

In this chapter, we will discuss the following topics:

- Introduction to Metrics Exporters
- Node Exporter
    - Key Features and Use Cases of Prometheus Node Exporter
    - Prometheus and Node Exporter Installation

- BlackBox Exporter
  - Key Features and Use Cases of Prometheus BlackBox Exporter
  - Installation and Usage of Blackbox Exporter
- WMI Windows Exporter
  - Key Features and Use Cases of Prometheus WMI Windows Exporter
  - Installation and Usage of WMI Windows Exporter
- My SQL Exporter
  - Key Features and Use Cases of Prometheus MySQL Exporter
  - Installation and Usage of MySQL Exporter
- cAdvisor Exporter
  - Key Features and Use Cases of Prometheus cAdvisor Exporter
  - Installation and Usage of cAdvisor Exporter

Introduction to Metrics Exporters

Metrics exporters are tools or components that extract and expose metrics from various sources in a format that Prometheus can scrape and ingest. These sources could be anything from server hardware, databases, cloud services, or custom applications. The exporters act as intermediaries, translating the raw metrics into a standardized format that Prometheus understands.

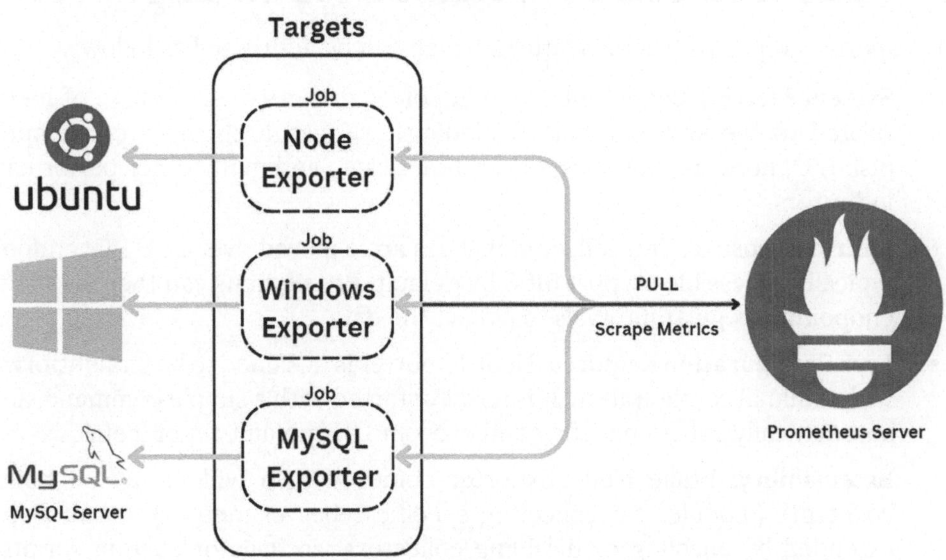

Figure 4.1: *Prometheus Metrics Exporters*

Exporters work by collecting data from their respective sources, which can include operating system metrics, application-specific metrics, network statistics, and more. Once collected, these metrics are exposed on an HTTP endpoint, typically in a plain text format. For instance, an exporter might make metrics available at a URL like `http://localhost:9100/metrics`. Prometheus then periodically scrapes these metrics by sending an HTTP request to the exporter's endpoint, with the scraped data subsequently stored in Prometheus' time-series database.

Now let us explore some of the widely used exporters. Let us start with Node Exporter. We will go through all the steps needed to install Prometheus and Node Exporter.

Node Exporter

Prometheus Node Exporter is an essential component of the Prometheus monitoring ecosystem. It is a software application designed to collect hardware and operating system-level metrics from *nix-based systems (such as Linux) and expose them in a format that Prometheus can scrape and store.

Node Exporter is primarily used for monitoring the health and performance of servers. It is commonly deployed on each server in an infrastructure, with Prometheus configured to scrape metrics from each instance. This setup allows for comprehensive monitoring of server fleets, helping operators detect and diagnose issues such as high CPU load, memory leaks, or disk space problems.

Key Features of Prometheus Node Exporter

Node Exporter comes with some features which can be addressed as follows:

- **System Metrics Collection**: Node Exporter gathers a wide range of metrics related to the system's state, including CPU usage, memory consumption, disk I/O, network statistics, file system usage, and many other performance indicators.
- **Metric Exposure**: The collected metrics are exposed over an HTTP endpoint, typically accessible on port 9100 by default. Prometheus can then scrape this endpoint at regular intervals to collect the data.
- **Less Configuration Required**: Node Exporter is designed to be straightforward with minimal configuration. It is usually started with a simple command, and it automatically starts collecting and exposing the default set of metrics.
- **Extensibility**: While Node Exporter comes with a wide range of built-in collectors (modules for collecting specific types of metrics), it can also be extended by enabling or disabling collectors via flags or custom scripts to gather additional metrics specific to your environment.
- **Lightweight**: The exporter is lightweight and optimized to have minimal

impact on the system it is monitoring, making it suitable for monitoring both large and small environments.

- **Open Source**: Prometheus Node Exporter is an open-source project under the Prometheus ecosystem, which means it benefits from community contributions and widespread usage across various environments.

Use Cases of Prometheus Node Exporter

By integrating the Node Exporter into a Prometheus-based monitoring stack, organizations gain comprehensive visibility into their infrastructure, enabling them to maintain reliability, optimize performance, and plan for growth effectively. Here are some common use cases:

- **System Resource Monitoring**: The Node Exporter tracks critical metrics such as CPU usage, memory utilization, disk I/O, and network bandwidth. These metrics are invaluable for understanding server performance and detecting potential bottlenecks.
- **Hardware Health Monitoring**: Metrics such as temperature, fan speed, and power usage can be exported (when supported) to monitor hardware health and identify potential failures before they impact operations.
- **Capacity Planning**: Historical data collected by the Node Exporter helps organizations forecast resource needs, plan upgrades, and ensure efficient utilization of hardware resources.
- **Performance Optimization**: By analyzing metrics related to system load, disk utilization, and process performance, administrators can identify areas for optimization and improve overall system efficiency.
- **Alerting and Incident Response**: With the Node Exporter feeding metrics into Prometheus, alerts can be configured to notify administrators of anomalies such as high CPU load, low disk space, or unusual network activity, enabling proactive issue resolution.

In the next section, we will begin demonstrating topics by exploring Node Exporter and its metrics. To do this, we will first need to install Prometheus.

Prometheus and Node Exporter Installation

This section will be a guide for Prometheus and Node Exporter installation and how they will be integrated to expose Node Exporter metrics from a Linux machine.

Prometheus Installation

The following steps show how to install Prometheus on a Linux system (for this demo,

I am using Ubuntu, but most steps are similar across other distributions). You can check possible installation options through this link.

1. **Update Your System**

   First, make sure your system packages are up to date.

   ```
   # apt-get update && sudo apt-get upgrade -y
   ```

2. **Create a Prometheus User**

   It is a good practice to run Prometheus as a non-root user. Create a dedicated user for Prometheus.

   ```
   # useradd --no-create-home --shell /bin/false prometheus
   ```

3. **Create Directories for Prometheus**

   Create necessary directories for Prometheus binaries, configuration, and data.

   ```
   # mkdir /etc/prometheus
   # mkdir /var/lib/prometheus
   ```

4. **Download Prometheus**

   Visit the Prometheus download page to find the latest version. You can use `wget` to download the package.

   ```
   # wget https://github.com/prometheus/prometheus/releases/down-
   load/v2.44.0/prometheus-2.44.0.linux-amd64.tar.gz
   ```

   Replace v2.44.0 and the corresponding filenames with the latest version if it has been updated.

5. **Extract the Package**

   Extract the downloaded tarball and move the necessary files.

   ```
   # tar -xvzf prometheus-2.44.0.linux-amd64.tar.gz
   # cd prometheus-2.44.0.linux-amd64
   # mv prometheus /usr/local/bin/
   # mv promtool /usr/local/bin/
   # mv consoles /etc/prometheus/
   # mv console_libraries /etc/prometheus/
   # mv prometheus.yml /etc/prometheus/
   ```

   The `promtool` binary is a command-line utility that provides tools for working with Prometheus. It can validate Prometheus configuration files and check the syntax of Prometheus expression language.

   The `consoles` and `console_libraries` directories contain templates and libraries for Prometheus rendering.

The `**prometheus.yml**` file is the main configuration file for the Prometheus server. It defines how Prometheus should discover and scrape targets, configure alerting rules, and set up various scrape configurations.

6. **Set Permissions**

   Make sure the Prometheus user owns the relevant directories and files.

   ```
   # chown -R prometheus:prometheus /etc/prometheus
   # chown -R prometheus:prometheus /var/lib/prometheus
   # chown prometheus:prometheus /usr/local/bin/prometheus
   # chown prometheus:prometheus /usr/local/bin/promtool
   ```

7. **Create a Systemd Service File**

   Create a `**systemd**` service file to manage the Prometheus service.

   ```
   # vi /etc/systemd/system/prometheus.service
   ```

   Add the following content to the file:

   ```
   [Unit]
   Description=prometheus
   Wants=network-online.target
   After=network-online.target

   [Service]
   User=prometheus
   Group=prometheus
   Type=simple
   ExecStart=/usr/local/bin/prometheus \
     --config.file=/etc/prometheus/prometheus.yml \
     --storage.tsdb.path=/var/lib/prometheus/ \
     --web.console.templates=/etc/prometheus/consoles \
     --web.console.libraries=/etc/prometheus/console_libraries

   [Install]
   WantedBy=multi-user.target
   ```

8. **Reload Systemd and Start Prometheus**

   Reload `**systemd**` to apply the new service and then start/enable Prometheus.

   ```
   # systemctl daemon-reload
   # systemctl start prometheus
   # systemctl enable prometheus
   ```

9. **Check Prometheus Status**

   Verify that Prometheus is running correctly.

   ```
   # systemctl status prometheus
   ```

You should see an active (running) status if everything is set up correctly.

10. **Access Prometheus Web Interface**

    Prometheus runs on port 9090 by default. You can access the Prometheus web interface by navigating to "**http://<your_server_ip>:9090**" in your browser.

11. **Configure Prometheus**

    The default configuration file is located at '**/etc/prometheus/prometheus.yml**'. You can configure Prometheus to scrape metrics from different targets and set up alert rules according to your monitoring requirements.

    ```
    # vi/etc/prometheus/prometheus.yml
    ```

    For now, let us add a new job to scrape metrics from node exporter, which will be installed in the next step. By default, node exporter exposes metrics on port **9100**, and because node exporter will be installed on the same machine where Prometheus is installed, we can use `**localhost:9100**` as the endpoint for the exposed metrics. Also, you can replace `**localhost**` with node IP.

    ```
    scrape_configs:
      - job_name: 'node_exporter_metrics'
        scrape_interval: 10s
        static_configs:
          - targets: ['localhost:9100']
    ```

`**Scrape interval**` determines how frequently Prometheus will scrape node exporter metrics.

Node Exporter Installation

To monitor the host system, you need to install Node Exporter, which exposes hardware and OS metrics as mentioned to Prometheus.

Run the given commands to install the node exporter binary:

```
# wget https://github.com/prometheus/node_exporter/releases/download/
v1.6.0/node_exporter-1.6.0.linux-amd64.tar.gz
# tar -xvzf node_exporter-1.6.0.linux-amd64.tar.gz
# mv node_exporter-1.6.0.linux-amd64/node_exporter /usr/local/bin/
```

You can replace "**1.6.0**" with the version you want to install.

Create a `**systemd**` service for Node Exporter similar to the one we created for Prometheus and start it. When you start Node Exporter service, you should be able to navigate to '**localhost:9100/metrics**' and see the exposed metrics within 10 seconds which is the scrape interval.

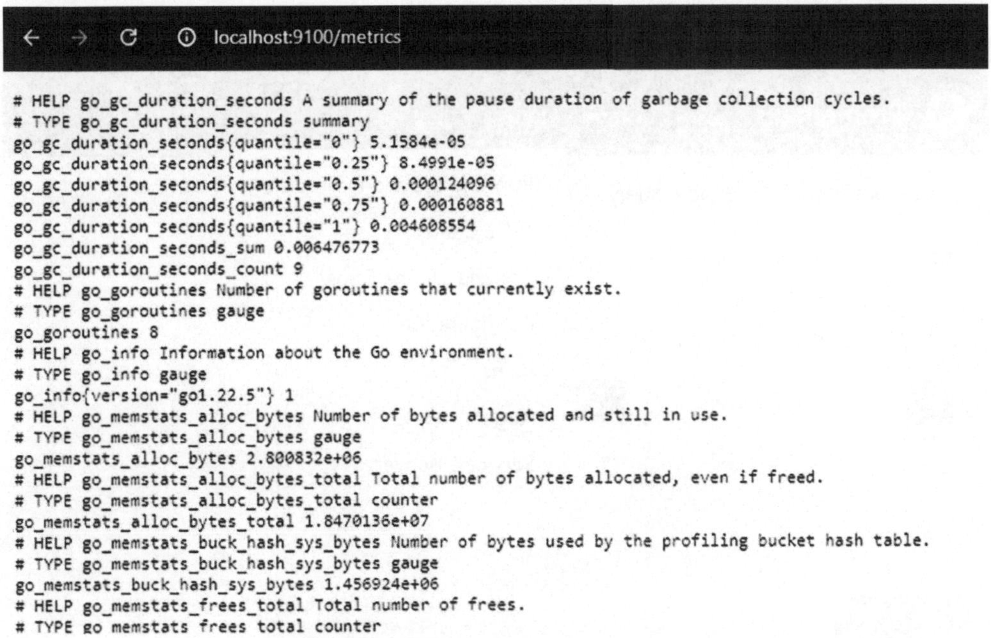

Figure 4.2: *Node Exporter Exposed Metric*

Example Metrics of Node Exporter

Here are some key example metrics that Node Exporter exposes:

- **CPU Metrics**
  - o **`node_cpu_seconds_total`**: Total amount of CPU time spent in various modes (user, system, idle, and others).
  - o **`node_cpu_seconds_total{mode="idle"}`**: Total CPU time spent in idle mode.
- **Memory Metrics**
  - o **`node_memory_MemTotal_bytes`**: Total amount of physical memory available.
  - o **`node_memory_MemFree_bytes`**: Amount of free physical memory.

Now when you navigate to Prometheus web UI, you can ensure that Prometheus is scraping the metrics from Node Exporter. Go to the "**Status**" > "**Targets**" page to see if the targets are up and running.

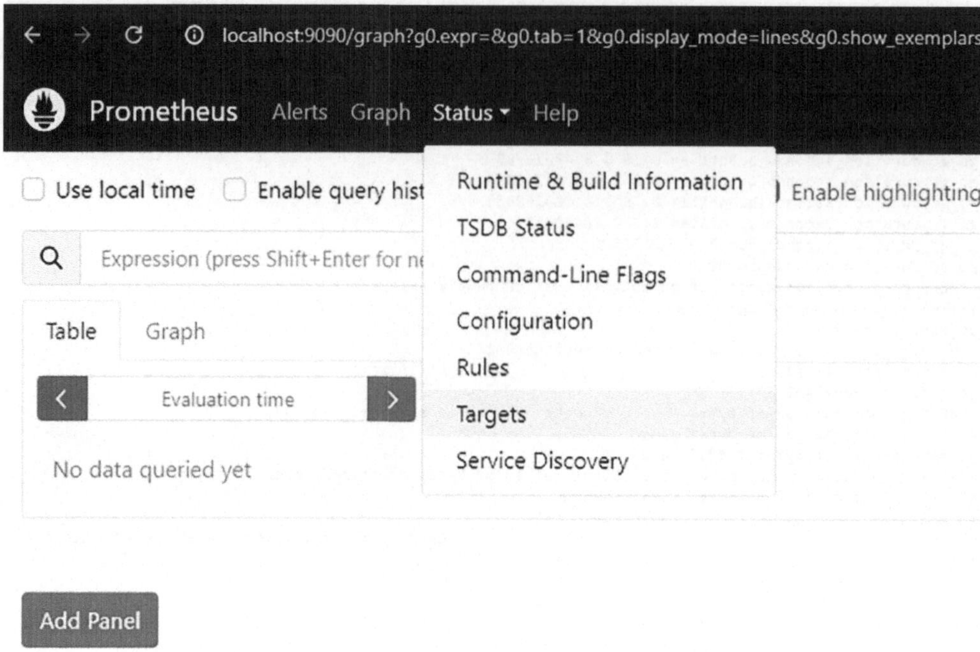

Figure 4.3: *Prometheus UI Status*

In *Figure* 4.4, you can see that Prometheus is successfully able to scrape the metrics exposed by the node exporter, and the state of the job is UP.

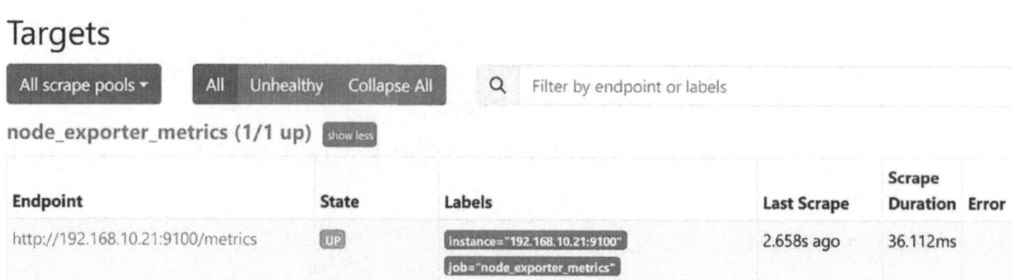

Figure 4.4: *Prometheus UI Targets*

For the upcoming sections, we will explore more Prometheus exporters. Most of the installation and integration steps are similar across different exporters, so we will not repeat those.

BlackBox Exporter

Prometheus Blackbox Exporter is a specialized tool within the Prometheus ecosystem designed for probing endpoints over various protocols to assess their availability, performance, and reliability. Unlike other exporters that gather metrics from specific services or systems, the Blackbox Exporter actively tests the reachability and responsiveness of endpoints from an external perspective.

You can download and install Blackbox Exporter through its github link: GitHub - prometheus/blackbox_exporter: Blackbox prober exporter.

Key Features of Prometheus Blackbox Exporter

Prometheus Blackbox Exporter comes with features to ensure effective performance monitoring of services across various network layers. Here are some of the key features:

- **Multi-Protocol Support**:
    - The Blackbox Exporter supports a variety of protocols for probing, including HTTP, HTTPS, DNS, TCP, and ICMP (ping). This flexibility allows it to monitor a wide range of services, such as websites, APIs, DNS servers, and network services.
- **Configurable Probes**:
    - Users can configure different types of probes depending on their needs. For example, an HTTP probe can check the status code of a response, measure response time, verify SSL certificates, or even search for specific content in the response body.
    - A "`probe`" refers to an active check or test that is performed on a service or endpoint to assess its availability, performance, and correctness.
- **Alerting on Availability**:
    - By using the Blackbox Exporter in conjunction with Prometheus, you can set up alerts based on the availability and response times of services. This makes it a powerful tool for monitoring service uptime and detecting outages.
- **External Monitoring**:
    - Blackbox Exporter is often used to simulate how users would interact with a service from the outside world, making it ideal for monitoring external-facing services or applications from an end-user perspective.
- **Detailed Metrics**:
    - The exporter provides detailed metrics on the probe results, including response times, DNS lookup times, and connection establishment times, which can help in diagnosing network or service issues.
- **Modularity**:
    - It is highly modular, allowing you to customize how each probe behaves.

For instance, you can define custom headers, POST data, or timeouts for HTTP probes, making it adaptable to various scenarios.

Use Case for Blackbox Exporter

By integrating the Blackbox Exporter into a Prometheus-based monitoring stack, organizations can gain a proactive approach to detecting and resolving service disruptions, ensuring high availability and reliability. The following are some of the common use cases:

- **Website Monitoring**: You can use the Blackbox Exporter to monitor the uptime and performance of websites. By configuring HTTP probes, you can track response times, ensure that SSL certificates are valid, and verify that specific content is being served correctly.
- **Service Availability**: For internal services, such as databases or API endpoints, Blackbox Exporter can be used to ensure that these services are reachable and performing within expected parameters.
- **DNS and Network Monitoring**: By probing DNS servers or network endpoints (using TCP or ICMP probes), you can ensure that the underlying network infrastructure is functioning correctly and identify potential issues before they affect users.

Example Metrics of Blackbox Exporter

The Prometheus Blackbox Exporter provides a variety of metrics that give detailed insights into the availability and performance of probed endpoints. Here are some key example metrics:

- `probe_success`: Indicates whether the probe was successful or not.
- `probe_duration_seconds`: The total time taken by the probe, in seconds.
- `probe_dns_lookup_time_seconds`: The time taken for the DNS lookup phase, in seconds.
- `probe_ssl_earliest_cert_expiry`: The timestamp for the earliest SSL certificate expiration date in Unix time.
- `probe_http_redirects`: The number of HTTP redirects encountered during an HTTP probe.

Installation and Usage of Blackbox Exporter

The Prometheus Blackbox Exporter can be installed on any server that needs to perform the probes. Once installed, it runs as a service, exposing metrics on a specified HTTP endpoint (by default, localhost:9115/metrics). You configure it by defining probes in a YAML configuration file, specifying the targets and types of checks (for example, HTTP, TCP, ICMP) you want to perform.

WMI Windows Exporter

WMI Exporter (now commonly referred to as the **Windows Exporter**) is a monitoring tool designed for Windows operating systems. It collects metrics from a Windows machine using Windows Management Instrumentation (WMI) and exposes them in a format that Prometheus can scrape and use for monitoring and alerting purposes.

Key Features of WMI Windows Exporter

The following are some of the key features of WMI that demonstrate how WMI Windows Exporter is an important tool for organizations running the Windows infrastructure:

- **Metric Collection from Windows Systems**: The WMI Exporter collects a wide range of system and application metrics from Windows operating systems, including CPU usage, memory usage, disk I/O, network traffic, and more. It gathers these metrics by querying the WMI, which is a Windows feature that provides a standardized interface for accessing management data.
- **Comprehensive Coverage**: The exporter covers a broad set of metrics that are critical for monitoring Windows environments. This includes detailed insights into system performance, hardware health, and application-specific metrics (such as metrics from IIS, SQL Server, and more).
- **Modular Design**: The exporter is modular, meaning it uses various collectors that can be enabled or disabled based on what metrics you need to gather. For example, if you only want to monitor CPU and memory usage, you can disable the collectors for disk or network metrics.
- **Ease of Integration with Prometheus**: The metrics exposed by the WMI Windows Exporter are formatted in a way that Prometheus can easily scrape. Once Prometheus is configured to scrape the exporter's endpoint, you can visualize these metrics, set up alerts, and analyze system performance over time.
- **Customization**: You can customize the exporter by configuring which WMI queries are run and what data is collected. This allows you to focus on the most relevant metrics for your specific use case.
- **Open Source**: The WMI Exporter is an open-source project, which means it benefits from community contributions and ongoing development. It is widely used in the industry, especially in environments that heavily rely on Windows servers.

Use Cases for WMI Windows Exporter

The following use cases demonstrate the WMI Windows Exporter's value in maintaining the performance, security, and reliability of Windows-based infrastructure:

- **Server Monitoring**: The WMI Windows Exporter is commonly used to monitor Windows servers in environments where Prometheus is deployed as the primary monitoring solution. It provides critical insights into server health and performance, helping administrators detect and troubleshoot issues such as high CPU usage, memory leaks, or disk space exhaustion.
- **Application Monitoring**: In addition to system metrics, the exporter can also be configured to collect metrics from specific applications running on Windows, such as Microsoft SQL Server, IIS (Internet Information Services), or even custom applications that expose metrics through WMI.
- **Hybrid Environments**: For organizations running both Linux and Windows servers, the WMI Exporter enables a unified monitoring approach using Prometheus, allowing for consistent metric collection across different operating systems.

Example Metrics of WMI Windows Exporter

The WMI Windows Exporter provides various metrics that offer detailed insights into the performance and health of Windows systems. Here are some example metrics:

- `wmi_cpu_time_total`: The total amount of time the CPU spends in different states, such as user mode, kernel mode, idle, and others.
- `wmi_system_processor_queue_length`: The length of the processor queue, which can indicate CPU contention.
- `wmi_os_physical_memory_free_bytes`: The amount of physical memory currently available on the system.
- `wmi_network_adapter_bytes_received_total`: Total bytes received by network interfaces.

Installation and Usage of WMI Windows Exporter

The WMI Windows Exporter can be installed as a service on Windows servers. Once installed, it runs continuously in the background, exposing metrics on a specified HTTP endpoint (by default, localhost:9182/metrics), which Prometheus can then scrape.

My SQL Exporter

The MySQL Exporter is a tool that collects and exposes metrics from a MySQL or MariaDB database, making them available for monitoring by Prometheus. This exporter allows you to gain detailed insights into the performance, health, and operation of your MySQL databases by providing a variety of metrics related to query performance, resource usage, and other important aspects of database management.

Key Features of MySQL Exporter

MySQL exporter comes with key features that allow proactive monitoring and troubleshooting with databases. The following are some of the key features:

- **Comprehensive Metrics Collection**: The MySQL Exporter gathers a wide range of metrics from the MySQL server, including query execution times, connection counts, cache hit rates, replication status, and more. These metrics help database administrators monitor the performance and health of their databases in real-time.
- **Easy Integration with Prometheus**: MySQL Exporter is designed to work seamlessly with Prometheus. Once the exporter is configured and running, Prometheus can scrape the metrics it exposes, allowing you to create dashboards, set up alerts, and analyze trends over time.
- **Customizable Metrics**: The exporter is highly configurable, allowing you to choose which metrics to collect based on your specific needs. You can enable or disable certain metrics, set query patterns, and even add custom queries to gather additional data.
- **Support for Multiple Databases**: The MySQL Exporter can be configured to monitor multiple databases on a single MySQL server, or even across different servers. This makes it a versatile tool for environments with multiple database instances.
- **Open Source**: The MySQL Exporter is an open-source project, widely used in the industry, and maintained by the Prometheus community. It benefits from community contributions and ongoing improvements.

Example Metrics Collected by MySQL Exporter

The MySQL exporter provides various metrics that offer detailed insights into the performance and health of MySQL databases. Here are some example metrics:

- **Query Performance Metrics**:
    - `mysql_global_status_queries`: Total number of queries executed.

  - **`mysql_global_status_slow_queries`**: Number of queries that have taken longer than the **`long_query_time`** threshold to execute.
  - **`mysql_perf_schema_events_statements_total`**: Total number of statements executed, grouped by type (for example, **`SELECT`**, **`INSERT`**).
- **Connection Metrics**:
  - **`mysql_global_status_threads_connected`**: Number of currently open connections.
  - **`mysql_global_status_max_used_connections`**: Maximum number of connections used simultaneously.
- **Replication Metrics**:
  - **`mysql_slave_status_seconds_behind_master`**: The number of seconds the slave is behind the master in replication.
  - **`mysql_slave_status_slave_sql_running`**: Whether the slave SQL thread is running (1 = Yes, 0 = No).
- **Disk Usage Metrics**:
  - **`mysql_global_status_innodb_data_read`**: The amount of data read, in bytes.
  - **`mysql_global_status_innodb_data_written`**: The amount of data written, in bytes.

Installation and Usage of MySQL Exporter

The MySQL Exporter can be installed on the same server as your MySQL database or on a separate monitoring server. Once installed, it runs as a service and exposes metrics on a specified HTTP endpoint (by default, localhost:9104/metrics). Prometheus can then scrape this endpoint to collect and store the metrics.

cAdvisor Exporter

cAdvisor (short for Container Advisor) is a monitoring tool that provides insights into resource usage and performance characteristics of running containers. It is particularly useful in environments using Docker and Kubernetes. While cAdvisor itself is not a Prometheus exporter in the traditional sense, it natively exposes metrics in a format that Prometheus can scrape, making it a key component in container monitoring.

You can check cAdvisor download options either in Docker environment or Kubernetes environment through this github link: GitHub - google/cadvisor: Analyzes resource usage and performance characteristics of running containers.

Key Features of cAdvisor

cAdvisor offers key features that allow monitoring and analyzing containerized workloads. The following are some of the key features:

- **Container Monitoring**: cAdvisor monitors resource usage and performance metrics for each running container. This includes CPU usage, memory usage, network I/O, disk I/O, and more.
- **Support for Multiple Container Runtimes**: While cAdvisor is most commonly associated with Docker, it also supports other container runtimes like `rkt` and `containerd`.
- **Detailed Metrics**: cAdvisor provides detailed metrics for every container, including historical resource usage, which helps in understanding the performance characteristics over time.
- **Integration with Prometheus**: cAdvisor natively exposes its metrics at an HTTP endpoint (/metrics), which can be scraped by Prometheus. This makes it easy to integrate into an existing Prometheus-based monitoring setup.
- **Kubernetes Integration**: In Kubernetes environments, cAdvisor is often integrated directly into the kubelet, making it an essential part of the Kubernetes monitoring stack.

Example Metrics Exposed by cAdvisor

The cAdvisor exporter provides various metrics that offer detailed insights into the performance and health of containers. Here are some example metrics:

CPU Metrics

- **`container_cpu_usage_seconds_total`**:
  - **Description**: Total CPU time consumed by the container, in seconds.
  - **Use Case**: Monitor CPU usage across containers to identify resource-hungry containers.
- **`container_cpu_cfs_throttled_seconds_total`**:
  - **Description**: Total time duration for which the container has been throttled (CFS throttling).
  - **Use Case**: Detect containers that are being throttled due to CPU resource limits.

Memory Metrics

- `container_memory_usage_bytes`:
  - **Description**: Current memory usage by the container, in bytes.
  - **Use Case**: Track memory usage and detect containers that are nearing or exceeding their memory limits.
- `container_memory_max_usage_bytes`:
  - **Description**: Maximum memory usage by the container.
  - **Use Case**: Understand the peak memory usage of containers.
- `container_memory_failures_total`:
  - **Description**: Number of memory allocation failures.
  - **Use Case**: Identify containers that have encountered memory allocation issues.

Network Metrics

- `container_network_receive_bytes_total`:
  - **Description**: Total number of bytes received over the network by the container.
  - **Use Case**: Monitor network traffic to and from containers.
- `container_network_transmit_bytes_total`:
  - **Description**: Total number of bytes transmitted over the network by the container.
  - **Use Case**: Ensure that containers are transmitting data as expected and detect any anomalies.

Disk I/O Metrics:

- `container_fs_reads_bytes_total`:
  - **Description**: Total number of bytes read by the container from the filesystem.
  - **Use Case**: Monitor disk read operations to detect containers with high I/O activity.
- `container_fs_writes_bytes_total`:
  - **Description**: Total number of bytes written by the container to the filesystem.
  - **Use Case**: Identify containers that are writing large amounts of data to disk.

Filesystem Metrics:

- `container_fs_usage_bytes`:
  - **Description**: Current filesystem usage by the container, in bytes.
  - **Use Case**: Track disk space usage to prevent containers from filling up the disk.
- `container_fs_limit_bytes`:
  - **Description**: Total filesystem size allocated to the container.
  - **Use Case**: Monitor the allocated storage to ensure containers have sufficient disk space.

Installation and Usage of cAdvisor Exporter

cAdvisor can be deployed as a standalone Docker container or integrated directly into a Kubernetes environment. It runs as a daemon on the host system, collecting and exposing metrics for all running containers.

Conclusion

Prometheus exporters are vital components in the Prometheus monitoring ecosystem, acting as intermediaries that collect and expose metrics from various systems, services, and applications that do not natively provide Prometheus-compatible metrics. Each exporter is tailored to a specific type of service, whether it is an operating system, a database, a hardware component, or a custom application.

Metrics collected by Prometheus exporters are fundamental to building effective Grafana dashboards and setting up alerting capabilities.

In this chapter, we have explored Prometheus installation and how it can be integrated with Node Exporter. We have also learned about other common exporters such as BlackBox Exporter, WMI Windows Exporter, MySQL Exporter, and cAdvisor Exporter. However, there are a lot of other exporters for more and different functionalities. You can explore other exporters through Prometheus exporter's link: https://prometheus.io/docs/instrumenting/exporters/.

In the next chapter, we will explore the Service Discovery feature, which allows Prometheus to automatically scrape metrics from dynamic resources.

Points to Remember

- Prometheus Metrics Exporters act as intermediaries that collect and expose metrics from various systems and services in a format Prometheus can scrape.

- Exporters are essential for integrating Prometheus with external components such as operating systems, databases, and applications.
- Node Exporter is used to collect hardware and OS-level metrics from Linux systems (for example, CPU, memory, disk usage).
- BlackBox Exporter is used for endpoint probing (for example, HTTP, HTTPS, TCP, ICMP), helping monitor availability and latency.
- WMI Windows Exporter is designed to collect system metrics from Windows machines, leveraging Windows Management Instrumentation (WMI).
- MySQL Exporter exposes database-specific metrics, such as query counts, slow queries, and connections.
- cAdvisor Exporter provides container-level metrics, such as resource usage and performance of Docker containers.
- Each exporter typically runs as a separate service, exposing metrics on a specific endpoint (for example, /metrics) that Prometheus can scrape.

Multiple Choice Questions

1. What is the primary role of a Prometheus metrics exporter?
   a. To store metrics in a database
   b. To expose metrics in a format Prometheus can scrape
   c. To send alerts when metrics are abnormal
   d. To visualize metrics in a dashboard
2. Which Prometheus exporter is most suitable for collecting hardware and OS metrics from a Linux server?
   a. BlackBox Exporter
   b. cAdvisor Exporter
   c. Node Exporter
   d. WMI Exporter
3. Which exporter is used to monitor availability of network endpoints using HTTP, HTTPS, TCP, or ICMP?
   a. MySQL Exporter
   b. Node Exporter
   c. WMI Exporter
   d. BlackBox Exporter

4. What is the purpose of the Prometheus MySQL Exporter?
    a. To monitor Linux server metrics
    b. To gather container performance metrics
    c. To expose metrics from MySQL or MariaDB databases
    d. To probe network endpoints for availability
5. Which Prometheus exporter is used specifically for monitoring Windows systems?
    a. Node Exporter
    b. BlackBox Exporter
    c. WMI Windows Exporter
    d. cAdvisor Exporter
6. If you want to monitor Docker container metrics such as CPU and memory usage, which exporter would you use?
    a. Node Exporter
    b. cAdvisor Exporter
    c. MySQL Exporter
    d. BlackBox Exporter

Answers

1. b
2. c
3. d
4. c
5. c
6. b

CHAPTER 5
Prometheus Service Discovery Feature

Introduction

Service Discovery in Prometheus allows it to automatically detect changes in your infrastructure (such as new services, instances, or pods) without manual intervention. This is very powerful in dynamic environments, such as those using Kubernetes, where services and endpoints change constantly.

Prometheus uses Service Discovery mechanisms to find the targets it needs to scrape for metrics. Once discovered, Prometheus pulls metrics from these endpoints at regular intervals as configured.

This chapter will explore how the Service Discovery feature works in Prometheus, and the kinds of configurations that can be used with the feature. We will also demonstrate how Service Discovery works in a Kubernetes environment to discover different Kubernetes resources.

Structure

In this chapter, we will discuss the following topics:

- Defining Service Discovery in Prometheus
    - Discovered Labels versus Target Labels
    - Service Discovery Workflow
    - Example Use Cases Solved by Service Discovery
- Methods and Supported Sources for Service Discovery
- Service Discovery Demo

Defining Service Discovery in Prometheus

Service Discovery in Prometheus solves the problem of dynamically managing and discovering monitoring targets in highly dynamic environments. Traditionally, in static infrastructures, administrators had to manually configure monitoring tools to specify the targets (for example, servers, applications, or services) from which to scrape metrics. However, modern cloud-native, containerized, and microservices-based environments are dynamic, meaning thereby that services are frequently added, removed, or scaled automatically.

Before going through a workflow on how Service Discovery works, you need to understand what Discovered Labels and Target Labels are in Prometheus Service Discovery.

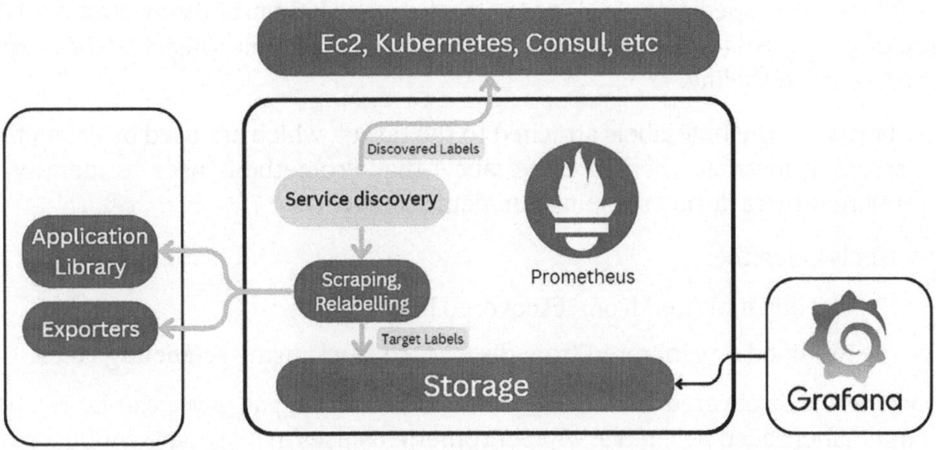

Figure 5.1: *Service Discovery Component in Prometheus Architecture*

Discovered Labels versus Target Labels

In Prometheus, **discovered labels** and **target labels** are both associated with service discovery, but they have different purposes in the context of monitoring targets. Understanding the distinction between these labels is important for correctly configuring Prometheus to scrape metrics from dynamically discovered services.

Discovered labels are metadata automatically assigned to targets by the service discovery mechanism. These labels are generated during the process of discovering services, nodes, or endpoints. Prometheus receives this metadata from the service discovery integration (for example, Kubernetes, Consul, or AWS EC2) and associates it with each target.

These labels often contain information about the discovered target, such as:

- IP address
- Instance ID
- Service name
- Region
- Labels/Tags (like those from Kubernetes pods or EC2 instances)

For example, in a Kubernetes environment, a pod might have discovered labels such as:

- `__meta_kubernetes_pod_name`
- `__meta_kubernetes_namespace`
- `__meta_kubernetes_pod_label_app`

These labels have a special **`prefix __meta_ to`** distinguish them as discovered labels and are not directly used for scraping. Instead, they are used for filtering and transforming the targets via relabeling.

Target labels are the final labels attached to the target, which are used by Prometheus when scraping metrics. These are the labels that Prometheus uses to identify and differentiate targets during scraping and data storage.

Target labels can either:

- Be directly inherited from discovered labels, or
- Be modified or generated from discovered labels using **relabeling rules**.

For instance, a discovered label like **`__meta_kubernetes_pod_name`** can be relabeled to a target label called **`pod_name`**, which Prometheus uses in its scrape configuration.

Service Discovery Workflow

In this section, we will review the service discovery flow in Prometheus.

1. **Service Discovery:** Prometheus discovers targets (such as pods, services, or instances) using a supported service discovery mechanism (for example, Kubernetes, Consul, EC2).

2. **Discovered Labels:** Each discovered target is assigned a set of metadata (discovered labels) such as **`__meta_kubernetes_pod_name`**, **`__meta_consul_service`**, **`__meta_ec2_tag_Name`**, and more.

3. **Relabeling:** Prometheus applies relabeling rules to the discovered labels. These rules are used to filter out irrelevant targets, modify the labels, or convert discovered labels into target labels.

4. **Target Labels:** After relabeling, Prometheus stores the final labels for the

target. These target labels are used when scraping metrics and stored in Prometheus along with the scraped data.

5. **Querying:** These target labels can be used in Prometheus Querying, and will also be used in data visualization in Grafana.

Example Use Cases Solved by Service Discovery

Service Discovery in Prometheus solves the critical challenge of monitoring dynamic, large-scale, and constantly changing infrastructures without manual intervention. Here are some of the use cases:

- **Kubernetes Pods**: In a Kubernetes environment, pods (which are often short-lived) are created and destroyed dynamically. Service Discovery ensures that Prometheus is always aware of the current state of the pods and automatically starts scraping metrics from new pods while stopping scraping when old pods are removed.
- **Auto-Scaling Groups**: In cloud environments, instances (for example, EC2 in AWS) may scale in and out depending on demand. Service Discovery ensures that Prometheus automatically tracks the new instances created by auto-scaling groups and removes instances that are terminated.
- **Microservices Environments**: Microservices architectures typically involve many services that communicate with each other and may change frequently. Service Discovery allows Prometheus to dynamically track which services are running and ensures they are continuously monitored without manual intervention.

Methods and Supported Sources for Service Discovery

Prometheus supports a variety of service discovery mechanisms to dynamically discover and monitor targets. These mechanisms allow Prometheus to automatically detect services, nodes, and instances without requiring manual intervention. Each service discovery mechanism is designed to integrate with specific infrastructure platforms, such as cloud providers, container orchestrators, or service registries.

Here is a detailed overview of the major service discovery mechanisms supported in Prometheus:

Kubernetes Service Discovery

Prometheus has built-in support for discovering resources in Kubernetes clusters, making it ideal for monitoring dynamic, containerized environments.

- **Resources Discovered**:
  - Pods
  - Nodes
  - Services
  - Endpoints
  - Ingresses
- **How it Works**: Prometheus interacts with the Kubernetes API to fetch metadata about running resources (for example, pods). Labels, annotations, and other metadata can be used to filter and relabel the discovered targets.
- **Configuration Example in YAML Format**:

```
scrape_configs:
  - job_name: 'kubernetes-pods'
    kubernetes_sd_configs:
      - role: pod
```

  Note: *`scrape_configs` section is part of the `prometheus.yml` file where we place the needed configuration for targets' metrics scraping and relabeling.*

- **Use Case**: Ideal for monitoring microservices running in Kubernetes, as it dynamically tracks new pods or services without manual intervention.

Consul Service Discovery

Consul is a widely used service registry and key-value store that helps microservices discover each other. Prometheus integrates with Consul to discover services registered within it.

- **Resources Discovered**:
  - Services
  - Instances registered in Consul
- **How it Works**: Prometheus queries the Consul API to retrieve a list of registered services and their instances. These instances are then monitored based on the provided metadata, such as IP addresses and ports.
- **Configuration Example in YAML Format**:

```
scrape_configs:
  - job_name: 'consul-services'
    consul_sd_configs:
      - server: 'localhost:8500'
```

- **Use Case**: Ideal for service-oriented architectures where Consul is used for service discovery and registration.

DNS Service Discovery

Prometheus can use DNS-SRV records to discover targets based on DNS queries, which is useful in traditional and cloud environments where services register themselves with DNS.

- **Resources Discovered:** Services or endpoints based on DNS records
- **How it Works:** Prometheus queries DNS for SRV or A records to discover the service targets. This is often used in load-balancing or failover setups where services dynamically register with DNS.
- **Configuration Example in YAML Format:**

```
scrape_configs:
  - job_name: 'dns-srv'
    dns_sd_configs:
      - names:
          - '_http._tcp.example.com'
```

- **Use Case**: Useful for environments where services use DNS for service discovery (for example, on-premise setups or cloud infrastructure relying on DNS).

Amazon EC2 Service Discovery

Prometheus supports **AWS EC2** service discovery to monitor instances running in Amazon Web Services (AWS) environments.

- **Resources Discovered**: EC2 Instances (VMs)
- **How it Works**: Prometheus queries the AWS EC2 API to list instances based on certain filters, like instance tags, regions, and availability zones. Prometheus can use instance metadata, such as instance IDs, tags, or private IPs, to discover targets.
- **Configuration Example in YAML Format**:

```
scrape_configs:
  - job_name: 'ec2-instances'
    ec2_sd_configs:
      - region: us-east-1
        filters:
          - name: "tag:Environment"
            values: ["production"]
```

- **Use Case**: Ideal for dynamically monitoring EC2 instances in auto-scaling groups, without requiring manual updates as instances are added or removed.

Google Cloud Platform (GCE) Service Discovery

Prometheus supports discovering instances running on **Google Compute Engine (GCE)** in Google Cloud.

- **Resources Discovered**: GCE VM instances
- **How it Works**: Prometheus uses the GCE API to discover instances based on certain filters, such as instance labels or machine types.
- **Configuration Example in YAML Format**:

```
scrape_configs:
  - job_name: 'gce-instances'
    gce_sd_configs:
      - project: 'my-gcp-project'
        zone: 'us-central1-a'
```

- **Key Use Case**: Used to monitor GCE virtual machines, especially in environments where new instances are frequently spun up or terminated.

Azure Service Discovery

Prometheus can dynamically discover resources running on **Microsoft Azure**, such as virtual machines and App Services.

- **Resources Discovered:**
  - Azure VMs
  - Scale Sets
- **How it Works**: Prometheus queries the Azure API to discover VMs based on resource group, region, or instance tags.
- **Configuration Example in YAML Format**:

```
scrape_configs:
  - job_name: 'azure-vms'
    azure_sd_configs:
      - port: 9100
        environment: AzurePublicCloud
        subscription_id: '<subscription-id>'
```

- **Use Case**: Ideal for environments running on Azure where VMs or scale sets are dynamically managed.

Marathon Service Discovery

Marathon is a container orchestration platform, often used with Apache Mesos. Prometheus supports discovering services deployed in Marathon.

- **Resources Discovered**: Marathon applications and tasks

- **How it Works**: Prometheus queries the Marathon API to retrieve the list of tasks or applications running within the Mesos cluster.

Configuration Example in YAML Format:

```
scrape_configs:
  - job_name: 'marathon-tasks'
    marathon_sd_configs:
      - servers:
          - 'http://marathon.mesos:8080'
```

- **Use Case**: Common in Mesos-based environments for monitoring dynamic, containerized applications.

Eureka Service Discovery

Eureka is a service registry often used in Netflix's microservices architecture. Prometheus integrates with Eureka to monitor services registered in its registry.

- **Resources Discovered**: Services registered in Eureka
- **How it Works**: Prometheus queries the Eureka API to retrieve the list of registered services and their instances, including metadata such as instance IDs, IP addresses, and ports.
- **Configuration Example in YAML Format**:

```
scrape_configs:
  - job_name: 'eureka-instances'
    eureka_sd_configs:
      - server: 'http://eureka-server:8080/eureka'
```

- **Use Case**: Ideal for monitoring microservices architectures where Eureka is used for service discovery and registration.

DigitalOcean Service Discovery

Prometheus supports service discovery for **DigitalOcean**, which is a cloud infrastructure provider.

- **Resources Discovered**: Droplets (VM instances)
- **How it Works**: Prometheus uses the DigitalOcean API to discover and monitor running droplets. Tags or metadata can be used to filter the instances that need to be monitored.
- **Configuration Example in YAML Format**:

```
scrape_configs:
  - job_name: 'digitalocean-droplets'
    digitalocean_sd_configs:
      - access_token: '<API_TOKEN>'
```

- **Use Case**: Useful for dynamically monitoring droplets in DigitalOcean environments.

Triton Service Discovery

Prometheus also supports service discovery for **Joyent's Triton** platform, which is used to run containers and build cloud infrastructure.

- **Resources Discovered**: Containers or virtual machines
- **How it Works**: Prometheus interacts with the Triton API to discover and monitor running instances.
- **Configuration Example in YAML Format**:

```
scrape_configs:
  - job_name: 'triton-instances'
    triton_sd_configs:
      - account: '<account>'
        dns_suffix: 'example.com'
```

- **Use Case**: Monitoring containers or VMs in Triton-based environments.

File-Based Service Discovery

Prometheus also supports a **file-based service discovery** mechanism, where targets can be dynamically discovered based on a list of targets defined in a file. This is useful for custom service discovery setups.

- **Resources Discovered**: Targets listed in a file (can be IP addresses, DNS names, or URLs)
- **How it Works**: Prometheus reads the target list from a file, which can be updated dynamically. The file can be periodically polled for changes.
- **Configuration Example in YAML Format**:

```
scrape_configs:
  - job_name: 'file-based'
    file_sd_configs:
      - files:
          - '/path/to/targets.json'
```

- **Use Case**: Custom service discovery where targets are not part of a standardized platform such as Kubernetes or Consul.

Service Discovery Demo

To demonstrate Service Discovery in Prometheus on Kubernetes, we will deploy Prometheus in a Kubernetes cluster and configure it to automatically discover and scrape metrics from various services and pods running within the cluster. To follow up on this demo, you should review the prerequisites that follow.

Prerequisites

- Up and running Kubernetes cluster. You can use minikube (https://minikube.sigs.k8s.io/docs/start/) or kind (https://kind.sigs.k8s.io/) to run a Kubernetes cluster in your local environment.
- Kubectl (https://kubernetes.io/docs/tasks/tools/) installed to interact with Kubernetes.
- Helm (https://helm.sh/docs/intro/install/) installed to deploy Kubernetes workloads.
- Basic knowledge of Kubernetes concepts (pods, services, and more)

Steps to Set Up Prometheus Service Discovery on Kubernetes

You can follow the steps below to install Prometheus on Kubernetes, then configure it for Service Discovery:

1. **Deploy Prometheus on Kubernetes:** We will use the official Prometheus Helm chart to install Prometheus in the Kubernetes cluster. This will simplify the deployment process.

   a. **Install Prometheus Using Helm:**

   Add the Prometheus community Helm repository:

   ```
   $ helm repo add prometheus-community https://prometheus-
   community.github.io/helm-charts
   $ helm repo update
   ```

   Install Prometheus in your Kubernetes cluster:

   ```
   $ helm install prometheus prometheus-community/prometheus
   ```

   This will install Prometheus with a default configuration that includes Kubernetes service discovery. You can check if the installation was successful by running:

   ```
   $ kubectl get pods -l app.kubernetes.io/name=prometheus
   ```

   You should see Prometheus-related pods running in the monitoring namespace:

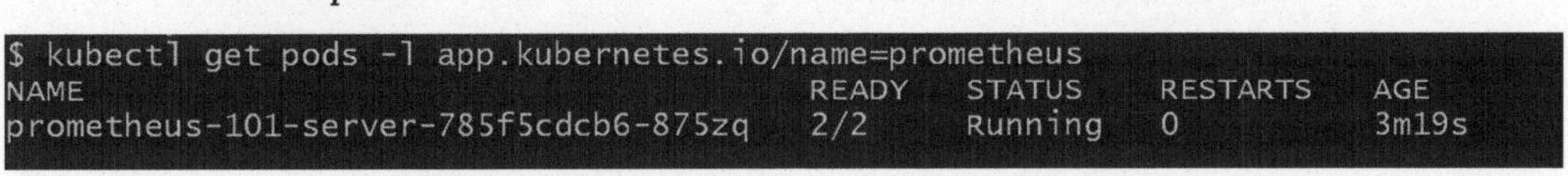

```
$ kubectl get pods -l app.kubernetes.io/name=prometheus
NAME                                   READY   STATUS    RESTARTS   AGE
prometheus-101-server-785f5cdcb6-875zq   2/2     Running   0          3m19s
```

Figure 5.2: *Prometheus Pods Up and Running*

b. **Access the Prometheus UI:**

To access Prometheus from your local machine, you can use the port-forward technique given further. You can also read about it through this link (https://kubernetes.io/docs/tasks/access-application-cluster/port-forward-access-application-cluster/):

```
$ kubectl port-forward svc/prometheus-server 9090:80
```

You can now access Prometheus at http://localhost:9090 in your browser.

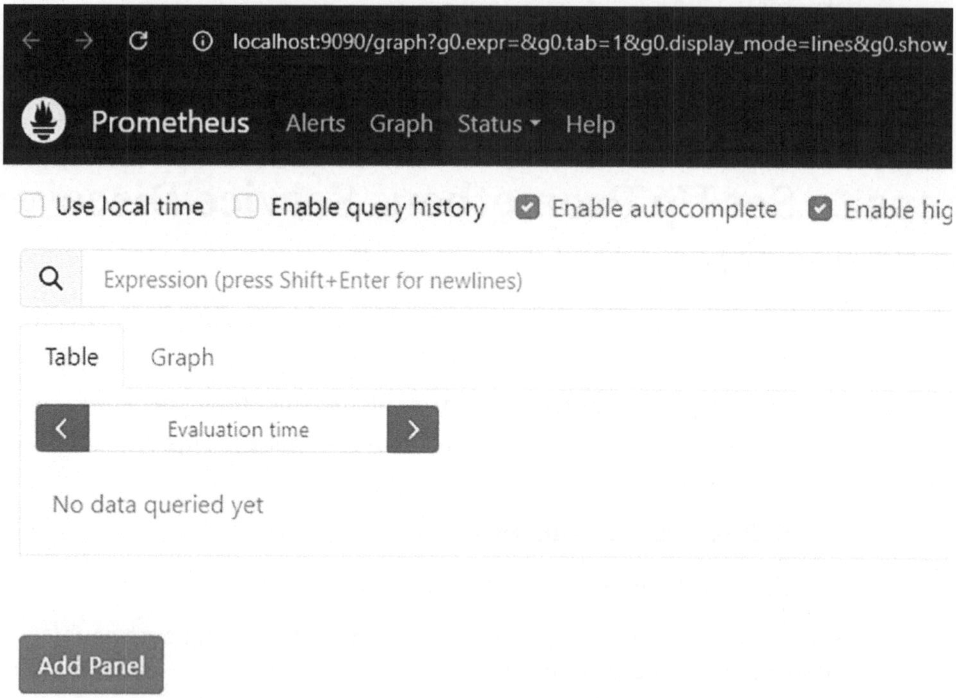

***Figure* 5.3**: *Prometheus UI*

Then you can navigate to **`Status`** > **`Service Discovery`** to check all Prometheus discovered resources.

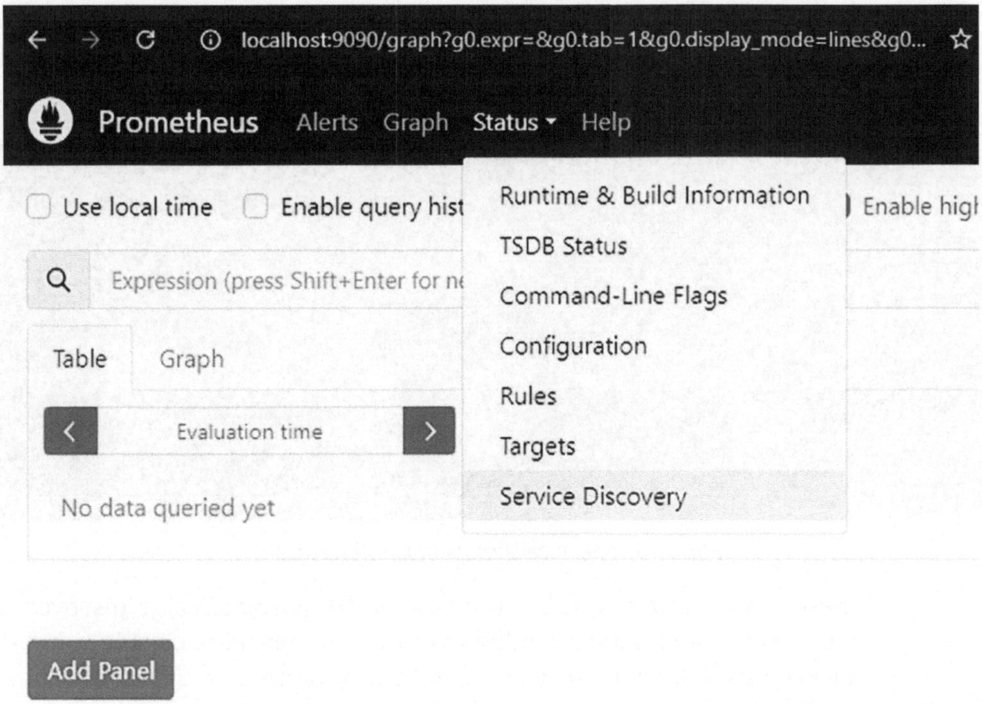

***Figure 5.4**: Prometheus Service Discovery UI*

2. **Configure Prometheus for Kubernetes Service Discovery:** Prometheus, by default, uses Kubernetes Service Discovery to discover targets (pods, nodes, services). You can see the discovery configuration by checking the **`prometheus.yml`** configuration.

   a. **View Prometheus Configuration:** The Prometheus configuration file (**`prometheus.yml`**) contains the scrape configurations, including the service discovery setup.

      You can view the **`ConfigMap`** used by Prometheus with the following command:

      ```
      $ kubectl get configmap prometheus-server -o yaml
      ```

      Look for **`prometheus.yml`** in the output. You will see sections as given under, which show how Prometheus is discovering services and pods:

      ```
      scrape_configs:
        - job_name: 'kubernetes-pods'
          kubernetes_sd_configs:
            - role: pod
        - job_name: 'kubernetes-nodes'
          kubernetes_sd_configs:
      ```

```
      - role: node
  - job_name: 'kubernetes-service-endpoints'
    kubernetes_sd_configs:
      - role: endpoints
```

```
job_name: kubernetes-pods
kubernetes_sd_configs:
- role: pod
relabel_configs:
- action: keep
  regex: true
  source_labels:
  - __meta_kubernetes_pod_annotation_prometheus_io_scrape
- action: drop
  regex: true
  source_labels:
  - __meta_kubernetes_pod_annotation_prometheus_io_scrape_
```

Figure 5.5: *Service Discovery Configuration*

These configurations tell Prometheus to automatically discover all pods, nodes, and service endpoints in the Kubernetes cluster using the Kubernetes API. Let us verify this in the next steps.

3. **Deploy a Sample Application in Kubernetes:** Now, let us deploy a sample application (for example, **nginx**) in 'default' namespace, then it is expected that Prometheus will discover the nginx pod as Service Discovery target, as it is already configured to discover all pods in the cluster.

   a. Deploy the NGINX Pod:

      Create a simple NGINX deployment and expose it as a service:

      ```
      $ kubectl create deployment nginx --image=nginx
      ```

   This will deploy an nginx pod in the '**default**' namespace.

   b. **Verify the Service Discovery:**

      Open Prometheus (http://localhost:9090), and navigate to **Status > Targets**. You should see the **nginx** pod listed in the **kubernetes-pods** section.

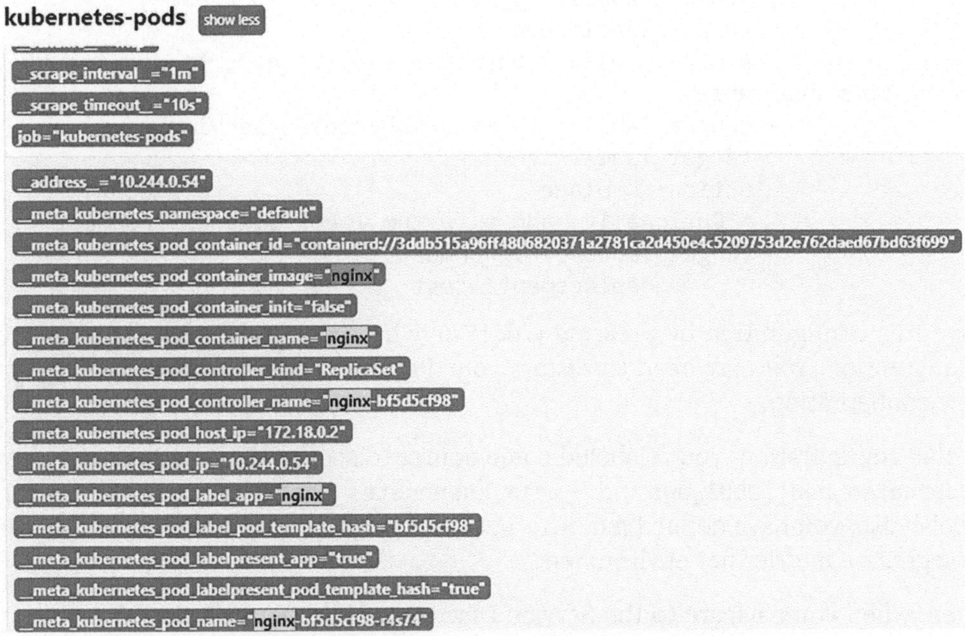

***Figure 5.6**: Service Discovery kubernetes-pods Job*

4. **Deploy a Custom Service Discovery Job in Kubernetes:** In this section, you will define a custom job to discover pods with specific relabeling configs.

   First, you need to edit the **`ConfigMap`** used by Prometheus to control Service Discovery with the following command:

   ```
   $ kubectl edit configmap prometheus-server
   ```

Then add a new job in the Service Discovery section as below. You need to take care of indentation while modifying the config map.

```
- honor_labels: true
  job_name: 'kubernetes-pods-custom'
  kubernetes_sd_configs:
    - role: pod
  relabel_configs:
    - source_labels: [__meta_kubernetes_pod_label_app]
      target_label: label_app
    - source_labels: [__meta_kubernetes_namespace]
      action: keep
      regex: default
      # Copy __meta_kubernetes_namespace to namespace
    - source_labels: [__meta_kubernetes_namespace]
      target_label: namespace
      # Copy __meta_kubernetes_pod_name to pod
```

```
          - source_labels: [__meta_kubernetes_pod_name]
            target_label: pod
            # Copy __meta_kubernetes_service_name to service if
it's available
          - source_labels: [__meta_kubernetes_service_name]
            target_label: service
            action: replace
            # Optionally, add a custom label like environment
          - target_label: environment
                   replacement: test
```

Save this configuration by pressing (**:wq!**) or whatever way you prefer to save the configuration. You may need to restart your Prometheus deployment to reflect the new configuration.

In this configuration, you relabeled some source-discovered labels such as **__meta_kubernetes_pod_label_app** and **__meta_kubernetes_namespace** to be used as target labels. Also, you have defined a new target label `environment' which could be useful to segregate metrics per environment.

Then, when you navigate to the Service Discovery page, you will notice the new job "**kubernetes-pods-custom**" created, and when you expand it, you will notice the target labels as configured.

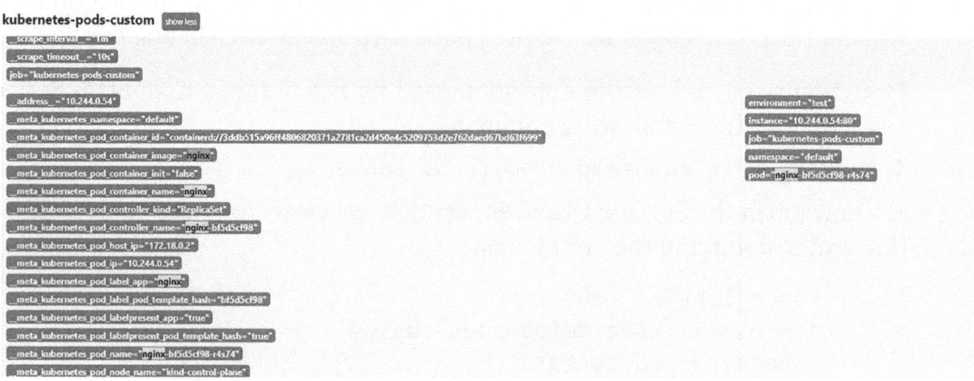

***Figure* 5.7**: *Service Discovery kubernetes-pods-custom Job*

5. **Access and Query Metrics in Prometheus (Optional):** Now that Prometheus is set up and service discovery is working, you can query metrics from the Kubernetes environment.

   Navigate to the "**Graph**" page in Prometheus and use the queries to review some metrics info.

   a. **Query Example for Nginx Container Info**:

   ```
   kube_pod_container_info{container="nginx", job="kubernetes
   -pods-custom", environment="test"}
   ```

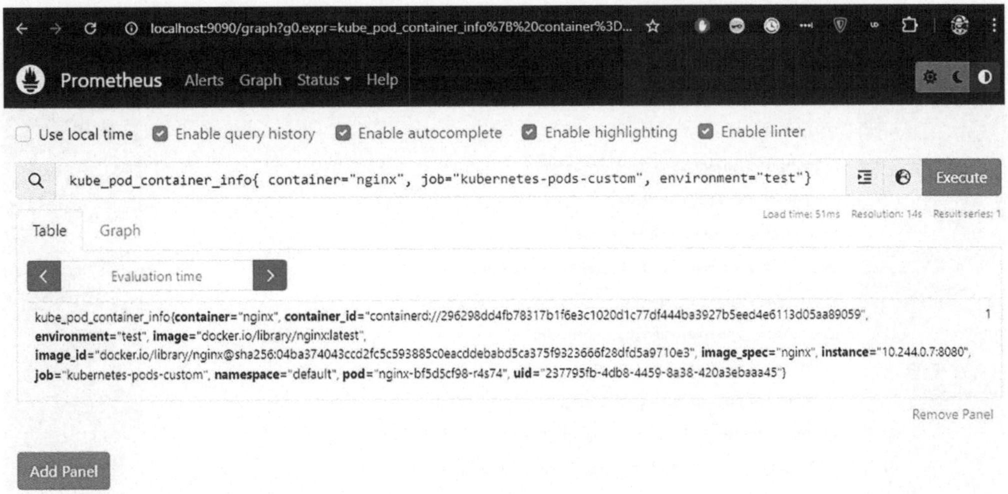

***Figure 5.8**: PromQL Query to Show Container Info*

b. **Query Example for Kubernetes Nodes**:

To monitor the nodes in your Kubernetes cluster, try the following query:

`up{job="kubernetes-nodes"}`

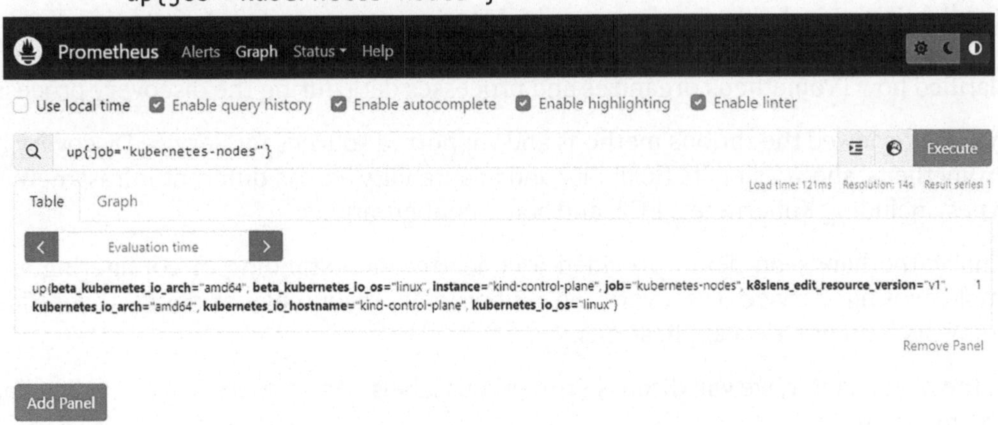

***Figure 5.9**: PromQL Query showing Kubernetes-nodes Job Status*

c. **Explore Different Metrics**:

You can explore all **`Prometheus metrics`** when you press the button next to the Execute button.

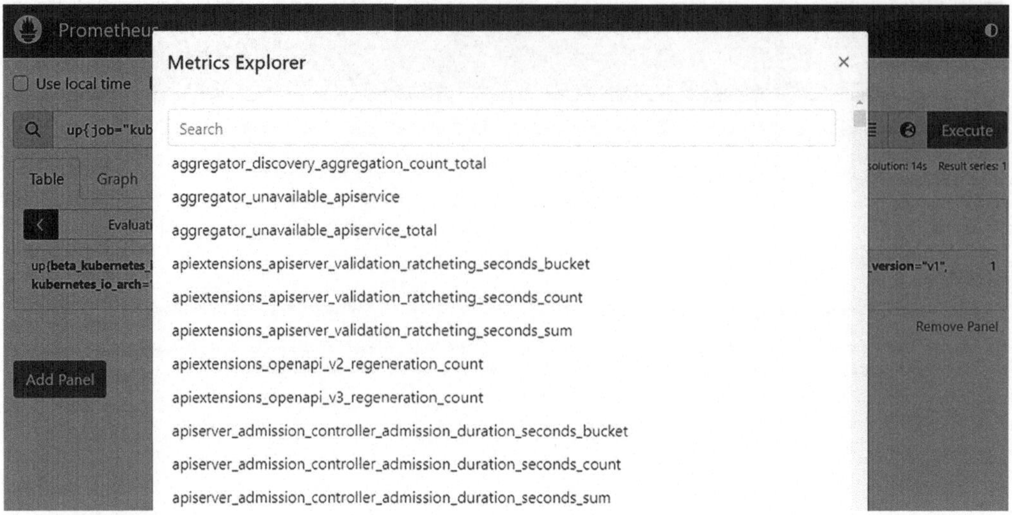

Figure 5.10: *Prometheus Metrics Explorer*

Conclusion

In this chapter, we explored the critical role of Service Discovery in Prometheus, highlighting its ability to dynamically identify and monitor targets in diverse environments. By distinguishing between discovered labels and target labels, we clarified how Prometheus organizes and processes data during the discovery process.

We also reviewed the various methods and supported sources for Service Discovery in Prometheus, showcasing its flexibility and adaptability across different infrastructure types, including Kubernetes, EC2, and static configurations.

Finally, the hands-on demo provided a concrete understanding of configuring and implementing Service Discovery on Kubernetes resources, bridging theoretical concepts with practical applications.

In the next chapter, we will discuss Prometheus labels and why labeling and relabeling are important.

Points to Remember

- Service Discovery in Prometheus enables automatic detection of targets (for example, services, instances, pods) to scrape metrics from, eliminating the need for manual configuration.
- It is especially beneficial in dynamic environments such as Kubernetes, where infrastructure elements are frequently created or destroyed.

- Prometheus uses pull-based scraping–once a target is discovered, it pulls metrics from the endpoint at regular intervals.
- Discovered Labels are metadata obtained from service discovery systems (for example, pod name, IP, namespace) and are prefixed with double underscores (__).
- Target Labels are the actual labels used by Prometheus when scraping metrics. You can map discovered labels to target labels using relabeling rules.
- Service Discovery Workflow involves:
  - Detecting endpoints using supported mechanisms
  - Applying relabeling to customize or filter targets
  - Regular scraping of valid targets
- Prometheus supports many service discovery mechanisms, including:
  - Kubernetes
  - Consul
  - EC2 (Amazon Web Services)
  - Azure
  - GCE (Google Cloud)
  - File-based SD (static file configs)
- Service Discovery allows Prometheus to scale seamlessly in cloud-native environments and microservices architectures.

Multiple Choice Questions

1. What is the primary benefit of using Service Discovery in Prometheus?
   a. It speeds up data visualization
   b. It allows Prometheus to send alerts directly
   c. It automatically detects and scrapes new targets
   d. It reduces the need for exporters
2. In Prometheus, what are discovered labels?
   a. Labels attached to time series data
   b. Labels defined in recording rules
   c. Metadata obtained from service discovery sources
   d. Labels used in Prometheus alerts

3. What is the function of relabeling in Prometheus service discovery?
   a. To compress time series
   b. To send data to other monitoring tools
   c. To map discovered labels to target labels
   d. To define alert thresholds
4. Which of the following environments most benefits from Prometheus Service Discovery?
   a. Static website hosting
   b. Kubernetes clusters
   c. Traditional on-premise infrastructure
   d. Desktop applications
5. Prometheus pulls metrics from targets based on what kind of model?
   a. Push
   b. Hybrid
   c. Pull
   d. Pull-and-push
6. What prefix do discovered labels in Prometheus typically have?
   a. @@
   b. __
   c. !!
   d. $

Answers

1. c
2. c
3. c
4. b
5. c
6. b

CHAPTER 6
Metrics Labeling and Relabeling

Introduction

One of the key features that makes Prometheus highly versatile is its labeling and relabeling mechanisms, which are fundamental for organizing and manipulating metrics data. Whether you are filtering out noisy metrics, standardizing labels, or ensuring efficient storage, labeling, and relabeling provide the flexibility to manage your metrics effectively and efficiently.

This chapter will explore labeling and relabeling in Prometheus, why they are essential, and how to implement them. You will also be given a practical demo in a Kubernetes environment, where you need to manage and clean up a lot of labels generated by dynamic workloads.

Structure

In this chapter, we will discuss the following topics:

- Understanding Prometheus Labels
- Understanding Prometheus Relabeling
    - Relabeling Rules in Prometheus
    - Key Reasons Why Relabeling Matters
- Demo: Relabeling Kubernetes Application Labels

Understanding Prometheus Labels

Labels in Prometheus are key-value pairs that are attached to metrics, providing additional context. Each metric can have several labels, making it easier to filter, aggregate, and analyze the data. For example, a metric **`http_requests_total`** might have labels such as **`method="GET"`**, **`handler="/api"`**, and **`status="200"`**.

Example:

```
http_requests_total{method="GET", handler="/api", status="200"}
http_requests_total{method="POST", handler="/api", status="500"}
```

In this example:

1. Method, handler, and status are labels.
2. The values GET, /api, and 200 are label values.

These labels allow you to slice and dice the metrics data according to specific dimensions, such as filtering all requests with a 500 status code.

Understanding Prometheus Relabeling

Relabeling in Prometheus is crucial for several reasons, especially in dynamic environments such as Kubernetes. It helps manage how metrics are collected, stored, and queried, ensuring that the monitoring system remains clean, efficient, and actionable.

Before moving to the key reasons as to why relabeling matters, let us review the relabeling rules and actions available in Prometheus. By understanding these rules, you will be able to apply different Prometheus relabeling rules to your configuration to serve a specific business need.

Relabeling Rules in Prometheus

In Prometheus, relabeling rules allow you to manipulate labels on targets and metrics as they are being collected or before they are stored. These rules are defined in the Prometheus configuration file and can be applied during target discovery, metric scraping, or alerting. The available relabeling rules are based on a set of actions that determine how labels should be transformed.

1. **`replace`**
    - **Description:** Replace the value of a label with a new value, or create a new label if it does not exist.
    - **Common Use:** Standardizing label names or values.
    - **Example:** The following configuration will replace the 'env' label with 'environment' and the **`'prod'`** label value with **`'production'`**

    ```
    relabel_configs:
      - source_labels: [env]
        regex: 'prod'
        target_label: 'environment'
        replacement: 'production'
        action: replace
    ```

2. **keep**
   - **Description:** Keeps only the targets or metrics that match the specified criteria; all others are dropped.
   - **Common Use:** Filtering out unnecessary targets or metrics.
   - **Example:** The below configuration will keep all the metrics from port 8080 port and drop all the others.

   ```
   relabel_configs:
     - source_labels: [__address__]
        regex: '.*:8080'
        action: keep
   ```
3. **drop**
   - **Description:** Drops targets or metrics that match the specified criteria.
   - **Common Use:** Removing unwanted targets or metrics to reduce noise or save storage.
   - **Example:** The given configuration tells Prometheus to drop metrics from all targets related to '**blackbox**' jobs.

   ```
   relabel_configs:
     - source_labels: [job]
       regex: 'blackbox'
       action: drop
   ```
4. **labeldrop**
   - **Description:** Drops specific labels entirely from the metrics.
   - **Common Use:** Removing sensitive or unnecessary labels.
   - **Example:**

   ```
   relabel_configs:
     - regex: 'env|instance'
       action: labeldrop
   ```
5. **labelkeep**
   - **Description:** Keeps only the specified labels and drops all others.
   - **Common Use:** Retaining only the essential labels for analysis.
   - **Example:**

   ```
   relabel_configs:
     - regex: 'job|instance'
       action: labelkeep 6. labelmap
   ```
   - **Description:** Renames labels based on a regular expression pattern.
   - **Common Use:** Bulk renaming of labels.

- **Example:**

```
relabel_configs:
  - regex: '__meta_(.*)'
    replacement: 'meta_$1'
    action: labelmap
```

7. `lowercase`
   - **Description:** Converts the label value to lowercase.
   - **Common Use:** Standardizing label values to avoid case-sensitivity issues.
   - **Example:**

```
relabel_configs:
  - source_labels: [instance]
    target_label: instance
    action: lowercase
```

8. `uppercase`
   - **Description:** Converts the label value to uppercase.
   - **Common Use:** Similar to lowercase, for standardization in uppercase.
   - **Example:**

```
relabel_configs:
  - source_labels: [region]
    target_label: region
    action: uppercase
```

9. `hashmod`
   - **Description:** Applies a modulo operation on the hash of the label value, typically used for sharding or load distribution.
   - **Common Use:** Distributing scrape targets across multiple Prometheus instances.
   - **Example:**

```
relabel_configs:
  - source_labels: [__address__]
    modulus: 2
    target_label: shard
    action: hashmod
```

Key Reasons Why Relabeling Matters

After reviewing Prometheus relabeling rules, let us understand how applying these rules will affect the efficiency of Prometheus performance:

1. **Target Discovery and Control:** In environments such as Kubernetes, targets

(for example, pods, services, nodes) are constantly changing as they scale up or down or get redeployed. Prometheus' **`Service Discovery`** automatically discovers these targets, but it can lead to large amounts of unnecessary or noisy data. Relabeling allows you to **`filter and control`** the targets that need to be scraped, ensuring you only gather metrics from relevant sources.

Example: **Keep** action can be used to scrape metrics only from pods with specific labels, such as prometheus.io/scrape=true, while ignoring others.

```
relabel_configs:
  - source_labels: [__meta_kubernetes_pod_annotation_prometheus_
io_scrape]
    regex: true
    action: keep
```

2. **Noise Reduction:** Prometheus collects a lot of metadata (labels) from the environment. In Kubernetes, this includes labels such as pod name, namespace, annotations, and many others. Some of this metadata is unnecessary for metrics analysis, leading to **label bloat** and making queries more complex. Relabeling can **remove unwanted labels** or rename them to streamline your metrics.

   Example: Use the **`labeldrop`** action to remove unused or excessive labels, like pod annotations.

```
relabel_configs:
  - action: labeldrop
    regex: __meta_kubernetes_pod_annotation_.*
```

3. **Label Standardization:** Different teams, environments, or applications might have different naming conventions for labels. Without standardization, querying across different sets of data becomes difficult. Relabeling allows you to **standardize labels** by renaming them, making cross-service or cross-environment metrics querying more efficient.

   Example: Replace inconsistent label names like env with environment.

```
relabel_configs:
  - source_labels: [env]
    target_label: environment
    action: replace
```

4. **Efficient Storage and Query Performance:** Prometheus stores time series data with all the associated labels. When there are too many labels, or when labels are not meaningful (for example, timestamps or IDs that change frequently), it can result in **high cardinality**. High cardinality impacts Prometheus' storage efficiency and query performance, leading to increased resource usage and slower queries. Relabeling helps reduce

this cardinality by **dropping unneeded labels** or consolidating metrics into fewer time series.

Example: Dropping **unique but unimportant** labels such as pod IP addresses to reduce cardinality.

```
relabel_configs:
  - source_labels: [__meta_kubernetes_pod_ip]
    action: labeldrop
```

5. **Sharding and Load Distribution**: In large environments, it might be necessary to distribute the scraping load across multiple Prometheus servers. Relabeling can be used to **shard targets** and distribute them among Prometheus instances. This is achieved by hashing the target's labels and using **`hashmod`** to split targets across servers.

   Example: Distribute scraping tasks across two Prometheus instances using **`hashmod`** based on the target's IP address.

```
relabel_configs:
  - source_labels: [__address__]
    modulus: 2
    target_label: shard
    action: hashmod
```

6. **Customizing Metric Paths**: Prometheus assumes that targets expose their metrics on the **`/metrics`** endpoint by default. However, some services might expose metrics on different paths or ports. With relabeling, you can **dynamically configure custom metric endpoints** based on annotations or other labels.

   Example: This rule will match any annotation that defines a custom path and use that value to replace the default */metrics* path.

```
relabel_configs:
  - source_labels: [__meta_kubernetes_pod_annotation_prometheus_
io_path]
    action: replace
    target_label: __metrics_path__
    regex: (.+)
```

7. **Hiding Sensitive Information**

   In some cases, targets may have labels that include sensitive information, such as internal IDs, service tokens, or other private data. Relabeling can be used to **remove or anonymize sensitive labels**, ensuring that only necessary and non-sensitive metadata is stored.

Example: Remove internal IDs from the scraped labels.

```
relabel_configs:
  - source_labels: [internal_id]
    action: labeldrop
```

8. **Multi-environment Setup**: In environments where multiple stages or environments (for example, development, staging, production) share the same Prometheus instance, relabeling is important to **isolate and tag environments** properly. By adding labels like environment, you can separate metrics from different environments, making it easier to query and analyze data specific to each one.

   Example: Add the environment label dynamically to metrics based on Kubernetes namespaces.

```
relabel_configs:
  - source_labels: [__meta_kubernetes_namespace]
    target_label: environment
    action: replace
    regex: dev|staging|prod
```

9. **Flexible Label Manipulation**: Relabeling gives you fine-grained control over labels. You can **create custom labels** based on existing ones, combine labels, or extract parts of labels using **regex**. This allows you to adapt the labeling to suit your specific monitoring requirements.

   Example: Combine a namespace and **pod_name** label into a new instance label for better identification.

```
relabel_configs:
  - source_labels: [__meta_kubernetes_namespace, __meta_
kubernetes_pod_name]
    separator: '/'
    target_label: instance
    action: replace
```

10. **Enabling Complex Queries**: Effective labeling and relabeling allow you to build **more powerful and meaningful queries**. By ensuring that the right labels are in place and irrelevant ones are removed, you can run queries that provide deeper insights and visualizations into your environment's health and performance.

Demo: Relabeling Kubernetes Application Labels

In this demo, we will focus on configuring Prometheus to scrape Kubernetes application's metrics and apply relabeling to control how those metrics are structured, labeled, and stored.

We assume that Prometheus is already installed in your Kubernetes cluster and that a Flask application is already running and exposing metrics.

Prerequisites

- Up and running Kubernetes cluster.
- Prometheus already installed (via Prometheus Operator or a standalone Prometheus instance).
- An application running in Kubernetes that exposes metrics, annotated with the necessary scrape configurations.

Step 1: Identify the Application to Scrape

We have a Flask application running in Kubernetes that exposes metrics via the **`/metrics`** endpoint, and we have annotated the pod or service to allow Prometheus to scrape it.

Here is an example of a running Kubernetes deployment in YAML with the necessary Prometheus annotations:

```
apiVersion: apps/v1
kind: Deployment
metadata:
  name: flask-app
  labels:
    app: flask-app
spec:
  replicas: 1
  selector:
    matchLabels:
      app: flask-app
  template:
    metadata:
      labels:
        app: flask-app
      annotations:
        prometheus.io/scrape: "true"  # Tells Prometheus to
scrape this pod
        prometheus.io/port: "5000"    # The port on which metrics
are exposed
        prometheus.io/path: "/metrics" # The path from which
metrics are scraped
    spec:
      containers:
      - name: flask-app
```

```
            image: <flask-app-image>:latest
            ports:
            - containerPort: 5000
```

This deployment has the following annotations:

- **prometheus.io/scrape: "true"**: tells Prometheus to scrape metrics from this pod.
- **prometheus.io/port: "5000"**: defines the port where the metrics are exposed.
- **prometheus.io/path: "/metrics"**: defines the path from which metrics are exposed.

Step 2 : Configure Prometheus Scrape Config with Relabeling

In this step, we will add Prometheus configuration with relabeling techniques and explore how these rules impact metric collection and optimization.

Relabeling Configuration: Let us expand on our relabeling configuration. Here is an enhanced version that applies more rules for label management:

```
scrape_configs:
  - job_name: 'flask-app'                 # Name of the job
    kubernetes_sd_configs:
      - role: pod                         # Discover all pods in the cluster
    relabel_configs:
      - source_labels: [__meta_kubernetes_pod_annotation_prometheus_
io_scrape]
        action: keep
        regex: true                       # Only scrape pods with the
annotation 'prometheus.io/scrape=true'

      - source_labels: [__meta_kubernetes_namespace]
        target_label: namespace            # Add Kubernetes namespace as a
label

      - source_labels: [__meta_kubernetes_pod_name]
        target_label: pod                  # Add pod name as a label

      - source_labels: [__meta_kubernetes_pod_annotation_prometheus_
io_path]
        target_label: __metrics_path__   # Set the scrape path based on
the 'prometheus.io/path' annotation
        regex: (.+)

      - source_labels: [__meta_kubernetes_pod_annotation_prometheus_
io_port]
```

```
        action: replace
        target_label: __address__       # Replace the target address
with pod IP and port from 'prometheus.io/port'
        regex: (.+)
        replacement: $1

      - action: labeldrop
        regex: __meta_kubernetes_pod_annotation_prometheus_io_.* # Drop
unnecessary pod annotations to reduce clutter

      - action: labeldrop
        regex: __meta_kubernetes_pod_label_.*    # Drop excessive
Kubernetes pod labels
```

Explanation of the Relabeling Rules:

a. **Filter by `prometheus.io/scrape=true`**: The first rule ensures that Prometheus only scrapes the pods with the annotation **`prometheus.io/scrape=true`**. This avoids wasting resources on scraping non-essential pods.

   Without this rule, Prometheus would attempt to scrape every pod, which could overload the Prometheus server and unnecessarily collect unwanted data.

b. **Add namespace and pod labels**: Namespace label is derived from the Kubernetes metadata and is extremely useful for querying metrics from a specific namespace.

   A pod label is added to distinguish between different pods of the same application. This is useful when scaling applications across multiple replicas, as each pod will expose its own metrics.

c. **`Set __metrics_path__ dynamically`:** The third rule dynamically sets the metrics path from the **`prometheus.io/path`** annotation. This makes it flexible to scrape applications that expose metrics at different paths without having to hard-code them in the configuration.

d. **`Set __address__ dynamically`**: The next rule dynamically sets the target address (IP and port) from the **`prometheus.io/port`** annotation. This allows Prometheus to connect to the right port for scraping the metrics from the application.

   By dynamically setting the address based on the pod's metadata, this avoids hardcoding IP addresses or ports in the scrape configuration, making it more flexible and reusable.

e. **Drop unnecessary labels (`labeldrop`):** The final relabeling rules clean up the metrics by removing unnecessary pod annotations and Kubernetes labels, which might clutter the metrics and increase the cardinality. Dropping unused labels can save storage and improve Prometheus performance by reducing the number of unique time series.

Step 3: Apply the Prometheus Configuration

a. **Update Prometheus `ConfigMap`**: Assuming you are using a **`ConfigMap`** to manage the Prometheus configuration, update the configuration with the new scrape and relabeling rules.

```
$ kubectl apply -f prometheus-configmap.yaml
```

This command will apply the changes to the **`ConfigMap`** containing your Prometheus configuration.

b. **Restart Prometheus deployment**: To apply the new configuration, let us restart the Prometheus pods:

```
$ kubectl rollout restart deployment/<DEPLOYMENT_NAME> -l
app=prometheus
```

Step 4: Verifying the Metrics in Prometheus

Once the configuration is applied, you can verify if the scraping is working and see how the relabeling has affected the collected metrics.

a. **Access Prometheus UI**: Use **`kubectl port-forward`** to access the Prometheus UI:

```
$ kubectl port-forward svc/<PROMETHEUS_SERVICE_NAME> 9090:9090
```

Now, open your browser and navigate to http://localhost:9090.

b. Check Scraped Targets: Go to **`Status`** > **`Targets`** in the Prometheus UI. You should see the Flask application listed under the job name "**`flask-app`**". The targets should show as UP if Prometheus is successfully scraping the metrics from your application.

When you click the job, you should be able to see the discovered labels versus the target labels. The relabeled and the new labels like pod and namespace should be listed in the target labels.

c. **Query the Metrics**: In the Prometheus Graph section, you can query the metrics from your application. For example, use the up metric to check if Prometheus is scraping your app:

```
up{job="flask-app"}
```

This will return 1 if Prometheus is able to scrape the Flask app, otherwise 0 if it is down.

Conclusion

This chapter explored how labels organize and categorize metrics, and how relabeling can transform or refine them, hence allowing you to unlock the full potential of Prometheus in managing complex monitoring environments.

Relabeling rules enables you to tailor metric data to your specific needs, whether that is streamlining configurations, filtering unnecessary metrics, or aligning data with organizational conventions. This becomes especially critical in dynamic environments such as Kubernetes, where relabeling can simplify monitoring across ephemeral and diverse workloads.

The next chapter will explore Prometheus Query Language PromQL, starting with the basic structure of queries, and gradually moving into more complex features.

Points to Remember

- Labels in Prometheus are key-value pairs attached to metrics that provide context (for example, instance, job, region), allowing for detailed filtering, querying, and grouping.
- Labeling enables metrics to be distinguished by dimensions, such as hostname, service, or environment.
- Relabeling is the process of modifying, adding, or removing labels–often used in service discovery and target configuration.
- Relabeling is especially important in dynamic environments such as Kubernetes, where large numbers of labels are generated by workloads (for example, pods, containers).
- Relabeling rules define how labels are transformed before Prometheus begins scraping metrics or adding them to storage.
- Relabeling can be used to:
    - Filter out unnecessary targets or labels
    - Standardize label names and values
    - Anonymize or redact sensitive data
    - Route and organize metrics more efficiently
- Relabeling is applied in various stages:
    - Before scrape (for example, target label transformation)
    - After scrape (for example, metric label transformation)
    - During alerting and remote write configuration

- Prometheus relabeling uses YAML configuration with actions such as **`replace`**, **`keep`**, **`drop`**, **`hashmod`**, and **`labelmap`**.

Multiple Choice Questions

1. What is the primary purpose of labels in Prometheus?
   a. To store metric values
   b. To control scrape intervals
   c. To provide context and metadata to metrics
   d. To define alert thresholds
2. What is relabeling in Prometheus?
   a. Changing metric values after scraping
   b. Modifying labels before or after scraping for better management
   c. Compressing metric data
   d. Creating custom dashboards
3. In which environment is relabeling especially useful due to frequent changes and dynamic label generation?
   a. On-premise servers
   b. Kubernetes clusters
   c. Static websites
   d. Traditional databases
4. Which of the following is NOT a valid relabeling action in Prometheus?
   a. replace
   b. drop
   c. inject
   d. keep

5. What is a common reason to use relabeling?
    a. To reduce Prometheus memory usage
    b. To encrypt metric data
    c. To anonymize or standardize incoming labels
    d. To improve alerting accuracy only
6. Which file format is typically used for defining relabeling rules in Prometheus?
    a. JSON
    b. XML
    c. YAML
    d. INI

Answers

1. c
2. b
3. b
4. c
5. c
6. c

CHAPTER 7
Prometheus Query Language PromQL

Introduction

Prometheus Query Language (PromQL) is a powerful and flexible query language used to retrieve and manipulate time series data stored by Prometheus. As part of the Prometheus monitoring ecosystem, PromQL enables users to perform real-time queries, filtering, and aggregation on the huge amounts of metrics data that Prometheus collects. Whether you are trying to visualize metrics on a dashboard, set up alerts based on thresholds, or troubleshoot system performance issues, PromQL is the essential tool for interacting with the data.

This chapter will guide you through the fundamental concepts of PromQL, starting with the basic structure of queries, and gradually moving into more complex features like functions and aggregations. By the end of the chapter, you will have a comprehensive understanding of how PromQL works and be able to construct your own queries to effectively monitor and troubleshoot systems. You will also be familiar with the Histogram Quantile function in PromQL, its working and usage.

You can practice all PromQL queries in this chapter directly through a Prometheus interface with already exposed metrics or even via PromLens, which is an intuitive query builder for Prometheus.

Structure

In this chapter, we will discuss the following topics:

- Basic Concepts of PromQL
    - Time Series Data
    - Metrics Types
- Structure of PromQL Query
    - Basic Syntax

  - Using Labels to Filter Metrics
- Range Queries and Operators
  - Range Vectors
  - Arithmetic Operators
  - Comparison Operators
- Functions in PromQL
  - Aggregation Functions
  - Mathematical Functions
  - Functions for Working with Time Series Data
  - Time Functions
  - Special Functions
  - Histogram Quantile Function

Basic Concepts of PromQL

To understand PromQL, it is important to be familiar with the **basic concepts** that underpin its working and effective usage. These concepts provide a foundation for writing powerful queries that allow users to extract, analyze, and aggregate data.

Time Series Data

Prometheus stores data as time series, which consist of:

- **Metric Names**: These define the feature or characteristic being monitored, such as **`cpu_usage`**, **`memory_available`**, or **`http_requests_total`**.
- **Labels**: Labels are key-value pairs that help distinguish different instances of the same metric. For example, a label might specify which application, environment, or region a particular metric is coming from.
- **Timestamps**: Each metric has a timestamp that indicates when it was collected, allowing Prometheus to build a time series over different points in time.
- **Values**: These are the actual measurements or values associated with the metric at a given time.

Metric Types

Prometheus supports different types of metrics, each suited to a specific use case:

- **Counters**: Monotonic values that increase over time, such as **`http_requests_total`**.

- **Gauges**: Metrics that can go up and down, such as CPU usage or memory consumption.
- **Histograms**: Metrics that sample observations and count them in configurable buckets, useful for request durations or response sizes.
- **Summaries**: Similar to histograms but more detailed, providing percentiles and quantiles for observation samples.

Structure of a PromQL Query

PromQL allows users to interact with the time series data in flexible ways, using expressions that are made up of one or more of the following components:

- **Instant vector**: Represents a set of time series data at a single point in time.
- **Range vector**: Represents time series data over a period of time.
- **Scalar**: A single numerical value.
- **String**: A simple text string.

Basic Syntax

At its simplest, a PromQL query consists of the metric name. For example, querying **`http_requests_total`** will return all time series data for that metric at the current moment.

```
http_requests_total
```

This query retrieves the latest values of all **`http_requests_total`** time series across all labels.

Using Labels to Filter Metrics

Labels play a crucial role in PromQL. You can filter results by adding label matchers in curly braces:

```
http_requests_total{job="api-server", method="GET"}
```

In this example, only time-series where the job is "**`api-server`**" and the method is "**`GET`**" are returned. Label matchers allow filtering based on specific criteria, which can include:

- `=`: Exact match.
- `!=`: Not equal.
- `=~`: Regular expression match.
- `!~`: Does not match the regular expression.

Range Queries and Operators

In PromQL, range queries and operators are powerful tools for analyzing time series data over a period of time rather than just at a single point. Range queries allow you to work with multiple data points over a defined time range, making them ideal for calculating trends, rates, and other time-based statistics. Operators provide the ability to compare, aggregate, and manipulate this data effectively.

Range Vectors

A range vector allows you to retrieve data over a specific time period. Range queries are defined by appending a time duration to the metric name in square brackets:

```
cpu_usage[5m]
```

This query retrieves all **cpu_usage** data from the past five minutes for every time series. You can specify a variety of time units, such as s (seconds), m (minutes), h (hours), and d (days).

Arithmetic Operators

PromQL supports basic arithmetic operations to manipulate data. The following operators are supported:

- Addition: +
- Subtraction: -
- Multiplication: *
- Division: /

For example, you might want to calculate the ratio of two metrics:

```
node_memory_free / node_memory_total
```

This query calculates the fraction of free memory relative to the total memory available for each node.

Comparison Operators

PromQL also provides comparison operators such as <, >, <=, ==, != and >= to filter results based on thresholds. For example, to find time series where the CPU usage is greater than 80%:

```
cpu_usage > 0.80
```

Functions in PromQL

PromQL comes with a wide variety of functions that are designed to manipulate and extract meaningful insights from time series data. These functions are essential when you need to perform complex computations, aggregations, or transformations on your metrics. The following is a detailed explanation of all the main types of functions available in PromQL, grouped into different categories for clarity:

Aggregation Functions

Aggregation functions allow you to summarize or group time series data by combining values across multiple dimensions (labels) into a single result.

- **`sum()`**
  - **Purpose**: Calculates the total (sum) of values across time-series.
  - **Usage**:
    `sum(http_requests_total)`

  This query sums up all HTTP requests across all instances and labels.

- **`avg()`**
  - **Purpose**: Computes the average value across time series.
  - **Usage**:
    `avg(cpu_usage)`

  This calculates the average CPU usage across all time series.

- **`min()`**
  - **Purpose**: Returns the minimum value across time series.
  - **Usage**:
    `min(memory_available)`

  This finds the minimum available memory across all instances.

- **`max()`**
  - **Purpose**: Returns the maximum value across time series.
  - **Usage**:
    `max(disk_io_time)`

  This returns the maximum disk I/O time from all the time series.

- **`count()`**
  - **Purpose**: Counts the number of elements (time series) with a value.

  - **Usage**:
    `count(cpu_usage)`

  This counts how many different time series are reporting CPU usage.

- **`stddev()`**
  - **Purpose**: Calculates the standard deviation of values across time series.
  - **Usage**:
    `stddev(response_time)`

  This calculates the standard deviation of response times.

- **`stdvar()`**
  - **Purpose**: Computes the variance of values across time series.
  - **Usage**:
    `stdvar(request_duration)`

  This calculates the variance in request durations across time series.

- **`count_values()`**
  - **Purpose**: Counts the number of occurrences of each distinct value in time series.
  - **Usage**:
    `count_values("value", node_boot_time)`

  This returns the count of distinct boot times across nodes.

- **`bottomk()`**
  - **Purpose**: Returns the smallest k elements by value.
  - **Usage**:
    `bottomk(3, cpu_usage)`

  This returns the three time series with the lowest CPU usage.

- **`topk()`**
  - **Purpose**: Returns the largest k elements by value.
  - **Usage**:
    `topk(5, memory_usage)`

  This returns the five time series with the highest memory usage.

Mathematical Functions

Mathematical functions allow you to perform standard mathematical operations on your time series data. Here are some of these functions:

- **`abs()`**
    - **Purpose**: Returns the absolute value of each element.
    - **Usage**:
      ```
      abs(disk_free_bytes)
      ```

  This query converts any negative values in **`disk_free_bytes`** to positive.

- **`ceil()`**
    - **Purpose**: Rounds each value up to the nearest integer.
    - **Usage**:
      ```
      ceil(cpu_load)
      ```

  This rounds all **`cpu_load`** values up to the nearest integer.

- **`floor()`**
    - **Purpose**: Rounds each value down to the nearest integer.
    - **Usage**:
      ```
      floor(cpu_load)
      ```

  This rounds all **`cpu_load`** values down to the nearest integer.

- **`round()`**
    - **Purpose**: Rounds each value to the nearest integer or to a specified decimal place.
    - **Usage**:
      ```
      round(cpu_load, 0.1)
      ```

  This rounds **`cpu_load`** values to one decimal place.

Functions for Working with Time Series Data

These functions are specifically designed to work with time series and their temporal nature.

- **`rate()`**
    - **Purpose**: Computes the per-second rate of increase for counters over a time range. It is commonly used with metrics like counters that only increase (for example, HTTP requests).
    - **Usage**:
      ```
      rate(http_requests_total[5m])
      ```

  This calculates the per-second rate of HTTP requests over the last five minutes.

- **`increase()`**
    - **Purpose**: Calculates the total increase in a counter over a time range.

  - **Usage**:

    ```
    increase(http_requests_total[1h])
    ```

  This returns the total number of HTTP requests received in the past hour.

- **`irate()`**
  - **Purpose**: Similar to rate(), but calculates the per-second rate of increase based only on the two most recent data points, making it more sensitive to short-term spikes.
  - **Usage**:

    ```
    irate(http_requests_total[5m])
    ```

  This returns the instantaneous rate of HTTP requests based on the last two data points over five minutes.

- **`delta()`**
  - **Purpose**: Computes the difference between the first and last data points in a range vector, typically used for gauges that fluctuate over time (for example, CPU usage).
  - **Usage**:

    ```
    delta(cpu_usage[10m])
    ```

  This calculates the change in CPU usage over the last ten minutes.

- **`deriv()`**
  - **Purpose**: Computes the per-second derivative of the time series, useful for detecting trends and rates of change.
  - **Usage**:

    ```
    deriv(cpu_usage[1h])
    ```

  This calculates the rate of change (derivative) of CPU usage over the last hour.

- **`predict_linear()`**
  - **Purpose**: Performs linear prediction over a time range, often used to predict future trends.
  - **Usage**:

    ```
    predict_linear(cpu_usage[1h], 3600)
    ```

  This predicts the CPU usage one hour into the future based on the last hour's data.

- **`resets()`**
  - **Purpose**: Counts the number of times a counter has reset in a given time range.

- **Usage**:
  ```
  resets(http_requests_total[1d])
  ```

This counts how many times the HTTP request counter has reset over the last day.

Time Functions

Prometheus provides time-related functions to help you work with time in your queries.

- **`time()`**
  - **Purpose**: Returns the current Unix timestamp (in seconds).
  - **Usage**:
    ```
    time()
    ```

  This returns the current time as a Unix timestamp.

- **`day_of_month()`**
  - **Purpose**: Returns the day of the month for the current timestamp.
  - **Usage**:
    ```
    day_of_month()
    ```

  This returns the day of the month (for example, 1-31).

- **`day_of_week()`**
  - **Purpose**: Returns the day of the week for the current timestamp (0 for Sunday, 6 for Saturday).
  - **Usage**:
    ```
    day_of_week()
    ```

  This returns the day of the week as an integer (for example, Sunday = 0, Monday = 1).

- **`hour()`**
  - **Purpose**: Returns the hour of the day (0-23) for the current timestamp.
  - **Usage**:
    ```
    hour()
    ```

  This returns the current hour of the day.

- **`minute()`**
  - **Purpose**: Returns the minute within the hour (0-59) for the current timestamp.

  - **Usage**:
    `minute()`

  This returns the current minute within the hour.

- **`month()`**
  - **Purpose**: Returns the month of the year (1-12) for the current timestamp.
  - **Usage**:
    `month()`

  This returns the current month as an integer.

- **`year()`**
  - **Purpose**: Returns the year for the current timestamp.
  - **Usage**:
    `year()`

  This returns the current year.

Special Functions

The following are some other functions that could be used for specific aggregation and operations:

- **`label_replace()`**
  - **Purpose**: Replaces or modifies label values in a time-series.
  - **Usage**:
    ```
    label_replace(http_requests_total, "new_label", "$1",
    "instance", "(.*)")
    ```

  This adds or modifies a label **`new_label`** based on the instance label.

- **`absent()`**
  - **Purpose**: Returns a single time series with a value of 1 if no data matches the query, otherwise returns an empty result.
  - **Usage**:
    `absent(up{job="database"})`

  This returns 1 if no instance of the database job is up.

- **`absent_over_time()`**
  - **Purpose**: Similar to absent(), but checks for the absence of data over a specified time range.
  - **Usage**:
    `absent_over_time(cpu_usage[5m])`

  This checks if no data was recorded for **`cpu_usage`** over the last five minutes.

Histogram Quantile Function

The **histogram_quantile()** function in PromQL is a powerful tool used for estimating quantiles (for example, percentiles) from histogram metrics. It is often employed to analyze distributions of values, such as request durations, latencies, or response sizes, based on time series data stored as histograms. In this section, we will explore how **histogram_quantile()** works, what histograms are in Prometheus, and how you can apply this function effectively in different use cases.

Histogram in Prometheus

In Prometheus, a histogram is a type of metric that samples observations and groups them into buckets based on their value. Each bucket holds a count of how many times the observation fell into a particular range (defined by the bucket's upper bound). Histograms are ideal for tracking things like:

- Request durations
- Latency distributions
- Response sizes
- Resource usage metrics

Each histogram metric in Prometheus consists of multiple sub-metrics:

- **metric_name_bucket**: A time series for each bucket that counts observations falling within that bucket's range.
- **metric_name_sum**: A time series that tracks the sum of all observed values.
- **metric_name_count**: A time series that tracks the total number of observations made.

For example, a histogram for request durations (**request_duration_seconds**) could have buckets such as 0.1s, 0.3s, 0.5s, and 1.0s, which reflect ranges such as [0s - 0.1s], [0.1s - 0.3s], and so on.

Defining Quantile

A quantile is a value that divides a dataset into intervals containing a specific fraction of the data. The most commonly used quantiles are:

- **50th percentile (median)**: The value below which 50% of the data points fall.
- **90th percentile**: The value below which 90% of the data points fall.
- **95th percentile**: The value below which 95% of the data points fall.
- **99th percentile**: The value below which 99% of the data points fall.

For instance, if you are tracking request durations and calculate the 95th percentile, you are finding the request duration below which 95% of all requests are completed.

The histogram_quantile() Function

The **histogram_quantile()** function in PromQL estimates a quantile for a given histogram. It takes two parameters:

```
histogram_quantile(ϕ, rate(metric_name_bucket[time_range]))
```

- **φ (phi)**: The quantile you want to calculate. This should be a value between 0 and 1. For example:
  - φ = 0.5 for the 50th percentile (median).
  - φ = 0.95 for the 95th percentile.
- **rate(metric_name_bucket[time_range])**: The rate of change for the histogram buckets over a specified time range. The **rate()** function is typically applied here because it calculates the per-second increase in the bucket counts over the given time period.

The **histogram_quantile()** function then uses the bucket counts to estimate the value of the requested quantile.

Example of histogram_quantile(): Let us assume you are measuring HTTP request durations in seconds with a histogram metric named **request_duration_seconds_bucket**. This metric has several buckets, such as:

- `request_duration_seconds_bucket{le="0.1"}`
- `request_duration_seconds_bucket{le="0.5"}`
- `request_duration_seconds_bucket{le="1.0"}`

Here is an example of how you can use **histogram_quantile()** to calculate the 95th percentile for request durations over the last five minutes:

```
histogram_quantile(0.95, rate(request_duration_seconds_
bucket[5m]))
```

This query calculates the 95th percentile request duration, meaning it estimates the duration below which 95% of all requests fall, based on the data from the past five minutes.

Understanding How histogram_quantile() Works

The **histogram_quantile()** function works by interpolating between buckets. Here is a simplified version of how it does this:

1. **Cumulative Sum of Buckets**: Each bucket in a histogram has an upper bound

(le label), and the counts are cumulative. The count in each bucket tells us how many observations fell below that upper bound. For instance, if you have a bucket with le="0.5", and its count is 200, then 200 observations had values less than or equal to 0.5 seconds.

2. **Linear Interpolation**: When calculating a quantile, Prometheus identifies the bucket that contains the requested quantile value and then performs a linear interpolation between the bounds of that bucket to estimate the quantile.

For example, if you are calculating the 95th percentile and 80% of the data falls below the previous bucket (le="0.3"), while 98% falls below the current bucket (le="0.5"), Prometheus will interpolate the 95th percentile value within this bucket.

Practical Use Cases for `histogram_quantile()`

Here are two practical cases where **`histogram_quantile()`** is used:

- **Latency SLO (Service Level Objective) Monitoring:** One common use case for **`histogram_quantile()`** is monitoring latencies to ensure they meet your SLOs. For instance, you may have an SLO that states "*95% of requests should be completed within 300ms.*" You can track whether your system is meeting this SLO with a query like:

  ```
  histogram_quantile(0.95, rate(http_request_duration_seconds_
  bucket{job="api-server"}[5m]))
  ```

  This query estimates the 95th percentile of request durations for the api-server job over the past five minutes. If the result is greater than 0.3 (300 milliseconds), your SLO may be violated.

- **Analyzing the Distribution of Resource Usage:** Another use case is analyzing how a system resource, such as CPU or memory, is being utilized across different workloads. Suppose you are monitoring container CPU usage with a histogram metric **`container_cpu_usage_seconds_bucket`**. You can calculate the 99th percentile of CPU usage across all containers like this:

  ```
  histogram_quantile(0.99, rate(container_cpu_usage_seconds_
  bucket[5m]))
  ```

  This query gives you the estimated CPU usage value below which 99% of containers fall over the last five minutes.

Considerations

Listed here are a few points to be addressed while working with PromQL:

- **Bucket Boundaries Impact Accuracy**: The accuracy of the **`histogram_quantile()`** function is determined by the granularity of your buckets. If your histogram has widely spaced buckets (for example, [0.1, 0.5, 1.0]), the quantile interpolation may be less accurate because Prometheus can only estimate the quantile within those wide ranges.

To improve accuracy, it is crucial to define bucket boundaries that are closely spaced in the ranges you are most interested in. For example, if you care about latencies between 100ms and 300ms, having buckets such as 0.1s, 0.15s, 0.2s, 0.25s, and 0.3s will give you better accuracy for those quantiles.

- **Histograms versus Summaries**: Prometheus also provides a summary metric type that can directly compute quantiles on the client side (the application exporting the metrics). While summaries offer more precision, they come with trade-offs, such as higher memory consumption and a lack of flexibility in adjusting quantile boundaries later. Histograms with **`histogram_quantile()`** are often preferred in cases where flexibility and control over bucket boundaries are needed.

Conclusion

In this chapter, we have explored the foundational concepts and practical applications of PromQL, the powerful query language used for interacting with time series data in Prometheus. Starting with an understanding of the basic concepts of PromQL and the nature of time series data, we delved into the various metric types and how they structure data for effective monitoring and analysis.

To further enhance data manipulation and visualization, we explored arithmetic and comparison operators, which enable complex calculations and comparisons directly within queries. The chapter provided an in-depth look at the wide array of functions in PromQL, including aggregation functions for summarizing data, mathematical functions for advanced calculations, and time functions for temporal manipulation. Special attention was given to the histogram quantile function, which provides valuable insights into data distribution.

In the next chapter, we will explore alerts in Prometheus—their description and significance—and how they can be configured and silenced.

Points to Remember

- PromQL (Prometheus Query Language) is the query language used to extract and analyze time-series data stored by Prometheus.
- It allows for real-time queries, filtering, aggregation, and transformation of metrics data.
- PromQL is used in dashboards, alert rules, troubleshooting, and performance analysis.

- Metrics in Prometheus are stored as time-series data, identified by a metric name and label set.
- PromQL queries follow a consistent structure: **`metric_name{label_filters}`**
- Labels are key-value pairs used to filter or group metrics (for example, **`instance="server1"`**).
- Range queries (for example, [5m]) fetch values over time intervals and are used with functions like **`rate()`** or **`avg_over_time()`**.
- Arithmetic operators (+, -, *, /) and comparison operators (==, !=, <, >) allow metric manipulation.
- Aggregation functions (for example, sum, avg, max, min, count) help in grouping and summarizing metrics.
- Functions in PromQL enhance query flexibility (for example, **`rate()`**, **`increase()`**, **`irate()`**, **`abs()`**, **`timestamp()`**).
- The **`histogram_quantile()`** function is used to estimate quantiles from histogram metrics, for example, 95th percentile response time.
- Tools like PromLens provide a graphical way to build and test PromQL queries interactively.

Multiple Choice Questions

1. What is PromQL used for in the Prometheus ecosystem?
   a. Sending metrics
   b. Building dashboards only
   c. Querying and manipulating time-series data
   d. Exporting data to Grafana
2. What type of data does Prometheus store that PromQL queries?
   a. JSON logs
   b. Time-series data
   c. Event logs
   d. Configuration files
3. In a basic PromQL query, what are labels used for?
   a. Visual styling
   b. Formatting output

  c. Filtering and grouping metrics
  d. Defining scrape intervals
4. What does the rate(**`http_requests_total[5m]`**) function do?
  a. Calculates the average of all requests
  b. Displays current value of a counter
  c. Computes the per-second rate of increase over 5 minutes
  d. Subtracts requests from 5 minutes ago
5. Which PromQL function is used to estimate percentiles from histogram metrics?
  a. `avg_over_time()`
  b. `irate()`
  c. `histogram_quantile()`
  d. `quantile_avg()`
6. What does the following query return?

```
up == 0
```

  a. All services that are currently active
  b. All metrics with no labels
  c. All targets that are currently down
  d. All metrics with values less than zero
7. What are range vectors used for in PromQL?
  a. Filtering label sets
  b. Storing histogram data
  c. Representing time-series data over a time interval
  d. Grouping labels into arrays

Answers

1. c
2. b
3. c
4. c
5. c
6. c
7. c

CHAPTER 8
Alerts and Alert Receivers

Introduction

Prometheus alerting is essential for proactive system monitoring, allowing teams to detect and respond to issues before they escalate into outages or performance bottlenecks. By setting up alerts on specific conditions (like high memory usage or instance downtime), Prometheus enables engineers to stay informed about critical metrics and anomalies in real time. Integrated with **`Alertmanager`**, it ensures that alerts are routed to the right people and channels, helping maintain system reliability, minimizing downtime, and improving overall service quality. Effective alerting keeps teams ahead of potential problems, reducing operational risks and enhancing user satisfaction.

This chapter will guide you on how to set up and manage alerts in Prometheus, and cover essential concepts such as setting alerts, using labels and annotations, configuring **`Alertmanager`**, and managing alert behaviors such as routing, grouping, and silencing.

Structure

In this chapter, we will discuss the following topics:

- Understanding Alerts in Prometheus
    - Labeling Alerts
    - Annotations in Alerts
- Setting Alerts in Prometheus
    - Service Availability Alert
    - High CPU Usage Alert
    - High Memory Usage Alert
    - Low Disk Space Alert

- Using Template Variables in Prometheus
    - How Template Variables Work
    - Common Template Variables
    - Examples of Using Template Variables
- Prometheus **`Alertmanager`**
    - Functionality of **`Alertmanager`**
    - Prometheus Alert Receivers
    - Applying New Configuration in Prometheus
- Testing Alerts in Prometheus
- Silencing Alerts in Prometheus

Understanding Alerts in Prometheus

In Prometheus, an alert is a condition defined by a set of rules that triggers a notification when specific thresholds or criteria are met within monitored metrics. Alerts are created using alerting rules, which specify conditions in PromQL (Prometheus Query Language) that indicate potential issues in the system, such as high CPU usage, memory saturation, or service unavailability.

When an alert rule's conditions are evaluated as true (often for a defined period), Prometheus generates an alert event. This event can then be forwarded to **`Alertmanager`**, which handles the routing, grouping, and notification of the alert, ensuring it reaches the appropriate teams or channels (such as email, Slack, or webhooks).

Labeling Alerts

Labels in Prometheus are key to organizing and filtering alerts. Labels, defined as key-value pairs in each alert rule, allow users to assign metadata such as severity levels, team names, or application identifiers. By using labels, alerts can be categorized for better organization and more efficient routing. For instance, you might use labels such as severity: high, environment: production, or team: database.

Example:

```
labels:
  severity: warning
  team: backend
```

Annotations in Alerts

Annotations provide additional context to alerts, helping engineers understand the cause of an alert and impact quickly. Unlike labels, annotations are not intended for routing; instead, they supply descriptions and messages about the alert. Prometheus supports templating in annotations, allowing dynamic data insertion to make alert messages more informative. Annotations often include details such as a short summary, a description, and a runbook URL.

Example:

```
annotations:
  summary: "High memory usage on {{ $labels.instance }}"
  description: "Memory usage has exceeded the threshold on
instance {{ $labels.instance }}. Investigate possible causes."
  runbook: "https://example.com/runbooks/high-memory"
```

Setting Alerts in Prometheus

Setting alerts in Prometheus involves defining alerting rules in a configuration file, typically in **prometheus.yml** or a dedicated rules file. These rules allow you to specify the conditions under which an alert should be triggered, using PromQL expressions to monitor key metrics.

Alerts are configured using alerting rules that are defined in specific configuration files. Here is a breakdown of where to configure these alerts:

- **Primary Configuration File (prometheus.yml):** The main configuration file for Prometheus is **prometheus.yml**, where you specify global settings and paths to external files, including alert rules. In **prometheus.yml**, the **rule_files** section lists the paths to one or more files that contain alert rules. Additionally, **prometheus.yml** includes the configuration for connecting to **Alertmanager** to handle alert notifications:

  ```
  rule_files:
    - "alert_rules.yml"  # Custom file for alert rules
    - "/etc/prometheus/rules/*.yml"  # Directory with additional
  rule files
  ```

- **Alert Rules Files:** Alert rules are often defined in separate YAML files to keep configurations organized and manageable. These files are specified in the **rule_files** section of **prometheus.yml**, and they typically contain alert rule definitions.

  Example rule file structure:

  - **alert_rules.yml**: To define general alerting rules.
  - **/etc/prometheus/rules/**: A directory containing multiple rule files, allowing for modular configuration.

Each rule file contains specific alert definitions, for example, **high_cpu_alert.yml**, **disk_space_alert.yml**, or other files based on monitoring needs.

Setting Alerts

Setting alerts in Prometheus involves defining alerting rules in a configuration file (for example, **alert_rules.yml**). These rules allow you to specify the conditions under which an alert should be triggered, using PromQL expressions to monitor key metrics.

Here are a few alert definitions for common monitoring scenarios: service availability, CPU usage, memory usage, and disk space.

- **Service Availability Alert:** This alert is triggered when a service (an instance) is down, which means that it is unreachable or has stopped responding.

```
groups:
  - name: ServiceAvailability
      rules:
      - alert: InstanceDown
         expr: up == 0
         for: 5m
         labels:
           severity: critical
         annotations:
           summary: "Instance {{ $labels.instance }} is down"
           description: "The instance {{ $labels.instance }} has
been unreachable for more than 5 minutes."
```

Where:

a. **Condition**: **up == 0** checks if the service status is down.

b. **for**: Ensures the service is down for at least five minutes before triggering.

c. **Labels**: Marks the severity as critical.

d. **Annotations**: Provides context, including the instance name, to make troubleshooting easier.

e. **{{ $labels.instance }}**: Is a template variable which will be illustrated in the next section.

High CPU Usage Alert

This alert triggers when CPU usage exceeds a certain threshold (for example, 80%) over a sustained period, indicating possible resource saturation.

```
groups:
  - name: CPUUsage
      rules:
      - alert: HighCPUUsage
```

```
        expr: (100 - (avg by(instance) (rate(node_cpu_seconds_
total{mode="idle"}[5m])) * 100)) > 80
        for: 10m
        labels:
          severity: warning
        annotations:
          summary: "High CPU usage on {{ $labels.instance }}"
          description: "The CPU usage on instance {{ $labels.
instance }} has exceeded 80% for more than 10 minutes."
```

Where:

a. **Condition**: The expression calculates CPU usage by subtracting idle CPU time from 100.

b. **`for`**: The condition must hold for 10 minutes before alerting.

c. **Labels and Annotations**: Set a warning level with details about the instance and CPU usage.

d. **`{{ $labels.instance }}`**: Is a template variable which will be illustrated in the next section.

High Memory Usage Alert

This alert fires when memory usage on an instance goes above a defined threshold, indicating potential memory constraints.

```
groups:
  - name: MemoryUsage
      rules:
      - alert: HighMemoryUsage
        expr: (node_memory_MemTotal_bytes - node_memory_
MemAvailable_bytes) / node_memory_MemTotal_bytes * 100 > 85
        for: 10m
        labels:
          severity: warning
        annotations:
          summary: "High memory usage on {{ $labels.instance
}}"
          description: "The memory usage on instance
{{ $labels.instance }} has exceeded 85% for more than 10 min-
utes."
```

Where:

a. **Condition**: Checks if memory usage is above 85%.

b. **`for`**: Ensures high memory usage persists for at least 10 minutes.

c. **Labels and Annotations**: Adds a warning severity with details about the instance and memory usage.

d. **`{{ $labels.instance }}`**: Is a template variable which will be illustrated in the next section.

Low Disk Space Alert

This alert notifies when available disk space is below a specified threshold, helping prevent unexpected storage outages.

```
groups:
  - name: DiskSpace
      rules:
      - alert: LowDiskSpace
          expr: (node_filesystem_avail_bytes / node_filesystem_
size_bytes) * 100 < 15
          for: 15m
          labels:
            severity: critical
          annotations:
            summary: "Low disk space on {{ $labels.instance }}"
            description: "Disk space on instance {{ $labels.
instance }} is below 15% for more than 15 minutes."
```

Where:

a. **Condition**: Checks if available disk space is below 15% of total disk space.

b. **`for`**: Waits for 15 minutes to prevent alerts on short-term fluctuations.

c. **Labels and Annotations**: Marks it as critical and provides instance-specific disk space details.

d. **`{{ $labels.instance }}`**: Is a template variable which will be illustrated in the next section.

Using Template Variables in Prometheus Alerting

Template variables in Prometheus alerting are placeholders used in alert annotations and labels that dynamically inject context-specific information when an alert is triggered. They allow alerts to contain details about the specific conditions that caused the alert, such as the affected instance, metric values, and other labels, making it easier for users to understand and respond to alerts.

How Template Variables Work in Prometheus Alerting

Template variables use the syntax **`{{ }}`** to wrap expressions and are typically used within annotations or labels in alerting rules. When an alert triggers, Prometheus replaces these variables with actual values from the metric data that matched the alert rule conditions.

Common Template Variables

Following are the most common template variables used for alert definition:

1. **`$labels.<label_name>`**
    - Refers to the value of a specific label associated with the metric that triggered the alert.
    - Common labels include instance, job, or any custom label set in the Prometheus target configuration.
    - **Example**: **`{{ $labels.instance }}`** would be replaced by the specific instance (for example, IP address or hostname) that triggered the alert.
2. **`$value`**
    - Refers to the actual value of the metric when the alert condition was met.
    - Useful for including the metric's value in alert messages for quick insights.
    - **Example**: **`{{ $value }}`** might resolve to 85.5, indicating the CPU usage percentage when a high CPU alert was triggered.
3. **`$alertname`**
    - Refers to the name of the alert itself as defined in the alert field of the rule.
    - **Example**: **`{{ $alertname }}`** could resolve to **`HighCPUUsage`**, providing clarity on what the alert is for.
4. **`$labels` and `$externalLabels`**
    - **`$labels`**: A collection of all label key-value pairs associated with the alerting rule's metric.
    - **`$externalLabels`**: Contains any external labels defined in **`prometheus.yml`**, which can be added for identifying sources across multiple Prometheus instances.

Examples of Using Template Variables

- **Instance-Specific Alert Message**

  Including **{{ $labels.instance }}** in an alert helps to identify exactly which instance caused the alert:

```
groups:
  - name: InstanceAlerts
      rules:
        - alert: InstanceDown
          expr: up == 0
          for: 5m
          labels:
            severity: critical
          annotations:
            summary: "Instance {{ $labels.instance }} is down"
            description: "The instance {{ $labels.instance }}
has been unreachable for more than 5 minutes."
```

  In this example, when an instance goes down, **{{ $labels.instance }}** will be replaced with the actual instance identifier, such as 192.168.1.10:9100. This makes it clear which server or service is down.

- **Metric Value in Alert Description**

  Including **{{ $value }}** in an alert helps to convey the actual metric value at the time of the alert:

```
groups:
  - name: ResourceUsage
      rules:
      - alert: HighCPUUsage
        expr: (100 - (avg by(instance) (rate(node_cpu_seconds_
total{mode="idle"}[5m])) * 100)) > 80
        for: 10m
        labels:
          severity: warning
        annotations:
          summary: "High CPU usage on {{ $labels.instance }}"
          description: "CPU usage on {{ $labels.instance }} has
reached {{ $value }}%, which is above the 80% threshold."
```

  Here, **{{ $value }}** would be replaced by the current CPU usage percentage (for example, 85.5%) at the time of the alert, providing immediate insight into the severity of the issue.

- **Alert Grouping with $alertname**

  Using **`$alertname`** can be useful when creating generic alert descriptions or summaries, which will be described in detail in Alert Manager section:

```
annotations:
  summary: "Alert: {{ $alertname }}"
  description: "Alert {{ $alertname }} triggered by instance {{
$labels.instance }} with value {{ $value }}"
```

This helps make alerts more readable, especially in logs or for notifications, by standardizing the format.

Benefits of Using Template Variables

- **Enhanced Alert Context**: Adding dynamic information like instance name and metric value helps alert recipients quickly assess what went wrong.
- **Customizable Messages**: Tailored messages allow for more meaningful alert notifications, enabling teams to take action without needing further investigation.
- **Effective Routing**: With context-specific data, Alertmanager can also apply more effective routing and escalation rules based on labels like severity or instance.

Prometheus `Alertmanager`

Prometheus **`Alertmanager`** is a component within the Prometheus ecosystem designed to handle alerts generated by Prometheus servers. Its primary role is to receive, process, and manage alerts, ensuring they are efficiently routed to the right recipients through a variety of notification channels, such as email, Slack, PagerDuty, or custom webhooks.

Functionality of `Alertmanager`

In Prometheus, users define alerting rules that evaluate specific conditions over metrics data (for example, CPU usage over 90% for 5 minutes). When these conditions are met, Prometheus triggers alerts and marks them as "**`firing`**."

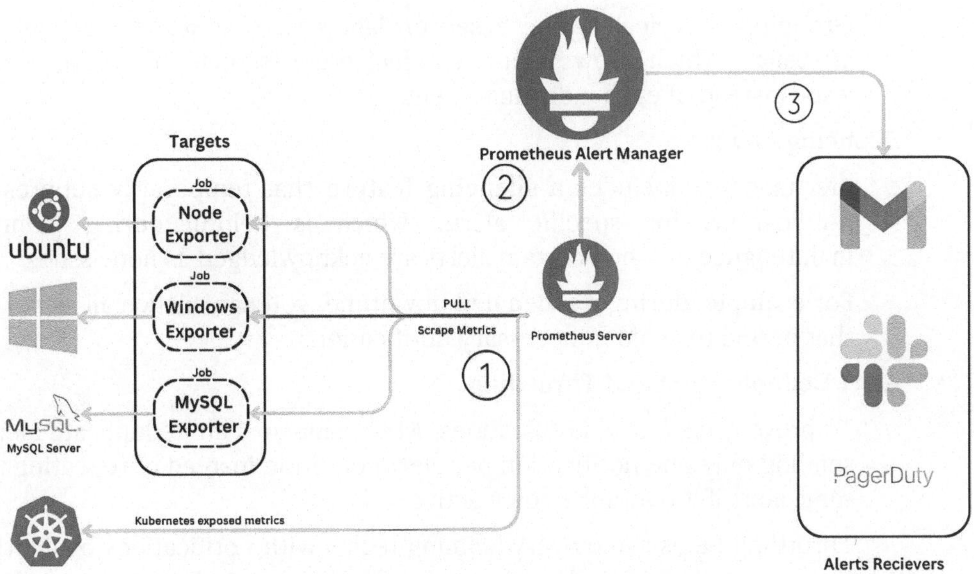

Figure 8.1*: Prometheus Alert Manager Diagram*

Once an alert condition is triggered, Prometheus sends the alert to Alertmanager for further handling. Prometheus continually checks the alerting rules, sending updates to **`Alertmanager`** on the status of alerts (such as "**`firing`**" or "**`resolved`**").

`Alertmanager` routes alerts based on a routing tree defined in its alert rules configuration files. This routing is based on labels associated with each alert (for example, severity, service, or environment) and can direct alerts to specific receivers (such as email, Slack, or PagerDuty).

Key Functions of Alertmanager

- **Routing Alerts to the Right Recipients**
  - **`Alertmanager`** allows you to set up rules to route alerts based on their labels (such as **`severity`**, **`instance`**, or **`alertname`**). This way, different types of alerts can be sent to the appropriate teams or individuals based on predefined conditions.

    For example, critical infrastructure alerts might go to the DevOps team, while application-specific alerts go to the development team.
- **Grouping Alerts for Manageability**
  - Alertmanager can group related alerts together, helping reduce the noise from multiple notifications for similar issues. For example, if multiple instances are experiencing high CPU usage, **`Alertmanager`** can combine them into a single grouped alert notification instead of sending a separate alert for each instance.

Grouping is typically done based on labels such as **`alertname`**, **`job`**, or **`instance`**, which allows teams to receive alerts that reflect the overall issue instead of each individual event.

- **Silencing Alerts**
  - Alertmanager includes a **silencing** feature that temporarily suppresses notifications for specific alerts, which is helpful during planned maintenance or when certain alerts are acknowledged as non-issues.

    For example, during a scheduled downtime, you can silence all alerts for that period to avoid unnecessary notifications.
- **Alert Deduplication and Throttling**
  - To prevent excessive notifications, **`Alertmanager`** can deduplicate alerts, sending only one notification per alert condition instead of repeating the same alert if it continues to be active.

    Throttling helps avoid overwhelming teams with notifications by limiting the frequency of alerts based on rules, ensuring that alerts are spaced out and manageable.
- **Escalation and Notification Policies**
  - **`Alertmanager`** allows teams to define escalation policies to determine what should happen if an alert is not acknowledged or resolved. For example, a critical alert might be sent to the primary on-call engineer, and if it is not acknowledged within a certain timeframe, it can be escalated to a senior engineer or the entire team.

    Custom notification policies can also be created to specify which channels should receive notifications based on alert types and severity.

`Alertmanager`'s configuration, defined in the **`alertmanager.yml`** file, is structured to manage alert routing, grouping, silencing, inhibition, and receivers for handling alert notifications. The configuration is modular and can be customized extensively to match specific alert management needs.

Key Sections of `Alertmanager` Configuration

- **Global Settings**
  - The global section defines general settings that apply to all notifications, such as default SMTP server configurations for email, Slack API URLs, and default notification frequencies.
  - These settings provide a centralized way to configure notification parameters that can be used across multiple receivers.

```
global:
  smtp_smarthost: 'smtp.example.com:587'
  smtp_from: 'alertmanager@example.com'
  smtp_auth_username: 'username'
  smtp_auth_password: 'password'
  slack_api_url: 'https://hooks.slack.com/services/T00000000/
B00000000/XXXXXXXXXXXXXXXXXXXXXXXX'
```

- **Route Configuration**
  - The route section is the core of **`Alertmanager`**'s routing mechanism. It defines how alerts are grouped, routed, and escalated based on various conditions.
  - The top-level route is the entry point for all alerts, and child routes can define further, more specific routing rules.

```
route:
  receiver: 'default-receiver'  # Fallback receiver if no
other route matches
  group_by: ['alertname', 'job'] # Group alerts by labels
  group_wait: 30s               # Delay before sending
grouped alerts
  group_interval: 5m             # Frequency to send
updates for active alerts
  repeat_interval: 1h            # Frequency to resend
notifications if alert remains active
```

Key Fields in Route Configuration

- **`receiver`**: Specifies the receiver that will handle alerts. If a specific alert matches no other route, it is sent to this fallback receiver.
- **`group_by`**: Defines how alerts are grouped; for example, grouping by **`alertname`** and **`job`** will send one notification for all alerts with the same name and job.
- **`group_wait`**: The delay before sending the first notification, allowing additional alerts to be grouped.
- **`group_interval`**: The minimum interval between sending notifications for a group of alerts.
- **`repeat_interval`**: The interval for resending alerts if the condition persists.

Nested Routes:

- The route configuration can contain child routes, which allows complex routing logic based on specific alert labels (such as severity, **`team`**, or **`alertname`**).
- Nested routes can be used for targeted routing, such as sending high-severity alerts to the primary on-call team while lower-priority alerts go to a secondary channel.

```
routes:
  - match:
      severity: 'critical'
      receiver: 'oncall-team'
      group_by: ['alertname', 'instance']
      group_wait: 10s
      group_interval: 2m
      repeat_interval: 30m

  - match_re:
      alertname: 'Node.*'
      receiver: 'ops-team'
```

- **Receivers**

  Receivers define the notification channels where alerts are sent, such as email, Slack, PagerDuty, or custom webhooks. Each receiver specifies the configuration for its respective channel.

  The receivers section lists all possible alert receivers, with each receiver having its specific notification configurations.

```
receivers:
  - name: 'email-notifications'
      email_configs:
      - to: 'team@example.com'

  - name: 'slack-alerts'
      slack_configs:
      - channel: '#alerts'
      send_resolved: true

  - name: 'pagerduty-notifications'
      pagerduty_configs:
      - service_key: 'PAGERDUTY_SERVICE_KEY'
```

Receiver Types:

- **Email**: Configures email recipients, SMTP server details (often set in global), and whether to send alerts once resolved.
- **Slack**: Configures Slack channels, message formatting, and resolution notifications.
- **PagerDuty**: Configures PagerDuty service keys, severity levels, and incident management options.
- **Webhook**: Configures custom webhooks, which can send alerts to other systems or custom alert-handling services.

- **Inhibition Rules**
  - Inhibition rules suppress alerts based on the presence of other, higher-priority alerts. This is useful for cases where one alert is a known cause for several downstream alerts, so only the primary alert should be notified.
  - Each rule specifies a **`source_match`** and **`target_match`** condition, so when the source condition is met, the target alerts are inhibited.

```
inhibit_rules:
  - source_match:
   severity: 'critical'
   target_match:
   severity: 'warning'
         equal: ['alertname', 'instance']
```

  In this example, if a critical alert for a particular instance is active, any warning alerts with the same **`alertname`** and *instance* are suppressed.

- **Silences**
  - Silences allow temporarily muting alerts that are expected or acknowledged, such as during maintenance periods.
  - Silences are not directly configured in **`alertmanager.yml`** but are managed through the **`Alertmanager`** web UI or API.
  - You can create a silence based on alert labels (for example, *instance*, *job*) and specify a duration, reason, and author.
- **Time Intervals**
  - **`Alertmanager`** supports time-based routing rules, which allow certain alerts to be sent to specific receivers only during designated time windows, useful for different handling during work hours versus after-hours.
  - Time intervals are set using the **`time_interval`** attribute.

Complete Configuration Example of `alertmanager.yml`

The following is an example of **`alertmanager.yml`** configuration file:

```
global:
  smtp_smarthost: 'smtp.example.com:587'
  smtp_from: 'alertmanager@example.com'
  smtp_auth_username: 'username'
  smtp_auth_password: 'password'
  slack_api_url: 'https://hooks.slack.com/services/T00000000/
B00000000/XXXXXXXXXXXXXXXXXXXXXXXX'
```

```
route:
  receiver: 'default-receiver'
  group_by: ['alertname', 'job']
  group_wait: 30s
  group_interval: 5m
  repeat_interval: 1h
  routes:
       - match:
       severity: 'critical'
       receiver: 'oncall-team'
       group_by: ['alertname', 'instance']
       group_wait: 10s
       group_interval: 2m
       repeat_interval: 30m
       - match_re:
       alertname: 'Node.*'
       receiver: 'ops-team'

receivers:
  - name: 'default-receiver'
       email_configs:
       - to: 'default@example.com'
  - name: 'oncall-team'
       email_configs:
       - to: 'oncall@example.com'
  - name: 'ops-team'
       slack_configs:
       - channel: '#ops-alerts'
       send_resolved: true

inhibit_rules:
  - source_match:
       severity: 'critical'
       target_match:
       severity: 'warning'
       equal: ['alertname', 'instance']
```

This configuration approach allows **Alertmanager** to provide flexible, powerful alert management tailored to specific needs, ensuring efficient incident response across diverse systems and teams.

Prometheus Alert Receivers

Prometheus **Alertmanager** supports a wide variety of alert receivers to route notifications to the appropriate channels. These receivers allow alerts to be sent through various means such as email, chat platforms, incident management tools, and custom webhooks.

Other Available Prometheus Alert Receivers

- **Opsgenie**
  - Sends alerts to Opsgenie for incident management.
  - Requires an API key to integrate with Opsgenie's alerting and on-call management services.
  - Alerts can include severity levels and additional fields to match Opsgenie's capabilities.

```
receivers:
  - name: 'opsgenie-alert'
   opsgenie_configs:
   - api_key: 'OPSGENIE_API_KEY'
                  send_resolved: true
```

- **Webhook**
  - Allows sending alerts to custom webhooks.
  - Webhook receivers are highly flexible and can be used to integrate with any external system that can handle HTTP POST requests.
  - Commonly used for custom alert handling and integration with other tools or scripts.

```
receivers:
  - name: 'webhook-alert'
   webhook_configs:
   - url: 'http://your-custom-webhook-url'
                  send_resolved: true
```

- **Pushover**
  - Sends alerts to Pushover, a mobile push notification service.
  - Requires a user key and API token for integration.
  - Useful for sending mobile alerts directly to individual or group devices.

```
receivers:
  - name: 'pushover-alert'
   pushover_configs:
   - user_key: 'PUSHOVER_USER_KEY'
         token: 'PUSHOVER_API_TOKEN'
```

- **Telegram**
  - Sends alerts to Telegram channels or individual users.
  - Requires a Telegram bot token and chat ID.
  - Can deliver alerts directly to Telegram for a quick view on mobile and desktop.

```
receivers:
  - name: 'telegram-alert'
   telegram_configs:
   - bot_token: 'TELEGRAM_BOT_TOKEN'
             chat_id: 'CHAT_ID'
```

Applying New Configuration in Prometheus

Prometheus provides an option to reload configuration files dynamically without requiring a full restart, which helps minimize downtime and improve efficiency.

Here is how it works:

1. **Prometheus Configuration Reload Endpoint**

    a. Prometheus can reload its configuration files (such as **`prometheus.yml`** and alert rule files) by sending a SIGHUP signal or by calling the reload endpoint at **`/-/reload`**.

    b. This endpoint triggers Prometheus to reload its configuration without restarting the entire service.

    ```
    curl -X POST http://localhost:9090/-/reload
    ```

    After running this command, Prometheus will apply the updated configuration immediately.

2. **Alertmanager Configuration Reload**

    a. Similarly, **`Alertmanager`** can reload its **`alertmanager.yml`** file without a restart.

    b. Use the same approach by sending a POST request to **`Alertmanager`**'s reload endpoint:

    ```
    curl -X POST http://localhost:9093/-/reload
    ```

    After running this command, Prometheus will apply the updated **`alertmanager`** configuration immediately.

Testing Alerts in Prometheus

Testing alerts in Prometheus is an essential step to ensure that alert rules and configurations in **`Alertmanager`** are set up correctly and will trigger notifications when real issues occur. Here are several methods for testing alerts in Prometheus:

- **Using the Prometheus Expression Browser (Manual Evaluation)**
    - Prometheus has an expression browser where you can manually evaluate alert expressions to see if they trigger as expected.

- Go to the Prometheus UI at **`http://<prometheus-server>/graph`**.
- Enter the alert expression in the query box and click Execute. This allows you to see if the condition is true (active) or false.
- If the query returns results (data points) that match your alert expression, the alert will trigger when the conditions are met.

- **Forcing Alert Conditions with Fake Data**
  - You can simulate alert conditions by creating fake data points in Prometheus.
  - Use the **`up`** metric or any other dummy metric, and adjust it to trigger an alert condition. For example, if your alert is set to trigger on high CPU usage, you could set up a temporary metric with high values to simulate this.
  - Adjusting metrics such as **`node_exporter`** or synthetic data can also be helpful for testing alert conditions in a more controlled environment.
- **Setting Alert Severity and Testing with Low Thresholds**
  - Lower the threshold for alert conditions temporarily to test if the alert fires.
  - For example, if an alert triggers when CPU usage is over 80% for five minutes, you can temporarily set it to 1% or a similar low threshold to ensure it fires.
  - After testing, reset the thresholds to the appropriate production values to avoid unwanted alerts in the live environment.
- **Testing Alerts in Alertmanager with amtool (Alertmanager CLI)**
  - **`Alertmanager`** comes with a command-line tool called **`amtool`** which allows you to test alert routes, silences, and other **`Alertmanager`** configurations.
  - You can use **`amtool`** to push test alerts to **`Alertmanager`** and observe how they are routed, grouped, or inhibited.
  - Example of sending a test alert:

```
amtool alert add testAlert severity=critical instance=test-in-
stance alertname="TestAlert"
```

  This helps validate **`Alertmanager`**'s routing and notification configuration.
- **Creating a Temporary Alert Rule in `alert_rules.yml`**
  - You can add a temporary alert rule with a condition that will always evaluate to true, such as a **`for`** clause with a very short duration, to quickly trigger the alert and test its configuration.

- **Example:**

```
groups:
  - name: TestAlertGroup
   rules:
   - alert: TestAlert
            expr: vector(1) == 1
            for: 1m
            labels:
              severity: critical
            annotations:
                 summary: "Test alert for validation"
```

This alert will always be **`true`**, causing it to trigger after one minute (based on the **`for`** clause) and sending it to **`Alertmanager`**.

After testing, make sure to remove this test rule to avoid unnecessary alerts.

Observing Alert States in the Prometheus UI

- Prometheus provides an Alerts tab in its UI where you can view the state of all configured alerts.
- Go to **`http://<prometheus-server>/alerts`** and monitor your alerts as they transition from inactive to pending and then to firing.
- This is a quick way to check which alerts are active and how they are changing in real-time.

Silencing Alerts in Prometheus

In Prometheus, alerts are silenced through **`Alertmanager`**. Silencing an alert means temporarily muting notifications for specific alerts based on conditions, without modifying the alert definitions themselves. This is useful during planned maintenance or when dealing with known issues to prevent unnecessary noise.

Methods to Silence Alerts in Alertmanager

- **Silences via the Alertmanager Web UI**
  - Navigate to the Alertmanager UI (usually *http://<alertmanager-server>*:9093).
  - Go to the Silences tab and click New Silence.
  - Define the silence parameters:
    - **Matchers**: Specify labels to match specific alerts you want to silence, such as alertname, instance, or severity.
    - **Duration**: Set the start and end time for the silence.

        - **Comment**: Add a reason for silencing the alert, helpful for tracking purposes.
    - **Example**: To silence all alerts from a particular instance (for example, web-server-01), you would set a matcher with instance: web-server-01.
- **Using `amtool` Silence Test**
    - If you want to test silence functionality in Alertmanager, you can create silences with amtool to verify that certain alerts do not trigger notifications.
    - Create a temporary silence that matches specific alert labels and verify that no notifications are sent while the silence is active.
    - Example to silence an alert through amtool:

```
amtool silence add severity=critical instance="test-instance"
alertname="TestAlert" --duration=1h
```

Conclusion

This chapter provided a comprehensive exploration of setting up and managing alerts in Prometheus, a critical aspect of monitoring and maintaining the health of your systems. We began by understanding the foundational concepts of alerts, including how they are structured with labels and annotations to provide context and clarity. We then reviewed configuration of various alert types, such as service availability alerts, high CPU and memory usage alerts, and low disk space alerts, thus ensuring that you can monitor essential system metrics effectively.

Additionally, we explored the use of template variables, which enable dynamic and reusable configurations for more flexible alerting setups. We demonstrated, through practical examples, how these variables streamline alert management across complex environments.

A significant part of the chapter was dedicated to the Prometheus Alert Manager, where we examined its role in managing alerts, routing them to appropriate receivers, and silencing non-critical alerts to reduce noise.

In the next chapter, we will review some advanced topics in Prometheus, such as securing Prometheus with TLS to ensure encrypted communication and protection of sensitive data, and implementing long-term storage for data archives.

Points to Remember

- Prometheus alerting allows for real-time detection of issues such as high resource usage or service downtime by evaluating metrics against defined conditions.
- Alerts are defined using PromQL expressions in Prometheus alerting rules.

- Each alert rule can include:
  - **Labels**: Metadata such as severity or environment for grouping and routing.
  - **Annotations**: Human-readable info such as summary or description of the alert.
- Prometheus does not send notifications directly. Instead, it forwards alerts to **`Alertmanager`**.
- **`Alertmanager`** is responsible for:
  - Routing alerts to the correct people or systems (for example, email, Slack, PagerDuty).
  - Grouping similar alerts to avoid noise.
  - Inhibition (preventing alerts if higher-priority ones exist).
  - Silencing (muting alerts for known issues or maintenance windows).
- Template variables (for example, **`{{ $labels.instance }}`**) are used in annotations for dynamic alert messages.
- You can define common alerts such as:
  - **Service Availability Alert**: if an instance is down (**`up == 0`**)
  - **High CPU Usage Alert**: if CPU usage exceeds a threshold
  - **High Memory Usage Alert**: for excessive memory consumption
  - **Low Disk Space Alert**: if disk usage is close to full
- After modifying alert rules or **`Alertmanager`** configuration, reload Prometheus or **`Alertmanager`** to apply the changes.
- Always test alerting rules using Prometheus's web UI or command-line before deploying to production.

Multiple Choice Questions

1. What is the main purpose of alerting in Prometheus?
   a. To visualize metrics
   b. To auto-scale services
   c. To detect and respond to system anomalies
   d. To replace manual deployments

2. What component is responsible for sending alert notifications in a Prometheus setup?
   a. Grafana
   b. PromQL
   c. Alertmanager
   d. Node Exporter
3. What is the function of annotations in a Prometheus alert?
   a. Define threshold conditions
   b. Route alerts to specific services
   c. Add human-readable messages to alerts
   d. Identify the scrape targets
4. Which PromQL expression would trigger an alert if a target is down?
   a. `up == 1`
   b. `up == 0`
   c. `cpu_usage > 80`
   d. `disk_free < 10`
5. What are template variables used for in Prometheus alerts?
   a. Automating configuration reloads
   b. Dynamically inserting label values into alert messages
   c. Scraping metrics faster
   d. Formatting metrics as JSON
6. What is the purpose of silencing an alert in **`Alertmanager`**?
   a. To permanently delete an alert rule
   b. To mute alerts temporarily during maintenance or known issues
   c. To log alerts only without sending notifications
   d. To increase the priority of critical alerts

7. What must be done after changing the Prometheus alert rules file?
    a. Restart the system
    b. Manually recompile Prometheus
    c. Reload the Prometheus configuration
    d. Restart **`Alertmanager`**

Answers

1. c
2. c
3. c
4. b
5. b
6. b
7. c

CHAPTER 9

Advanced Prometheus Techniques

Introduction

While the basics of Prometheus, such as setting up metrics, using PromQL for querying, and configuring alerts, are relatively straightforward, knowledge of advanced topics can significantly enhance your ability to monitor complex systems and optimize performance.

This chapter will guide you through advanced topics in Prometheus, such as securing Prometheus with TLS to ensure encrypted communication and protection of sensitive data, and implementing long-term storage for historical data to support trend analysis and compliance requirements. You will also learn about integrating Prometheus with other observability tools such as Grafana, Loki, Jaeger, Thanos, and OpenTelemetry, enabling a unified monitoring solution that combines metrics, logs, and traces for holistic insights.

Additionally, it covers essential strategies for capacity planning to prepare for scaling needs, performance tuning to optimize query efficiency and resource usage, and automating Prometheus deployment and management using tools such as Helm, Terraform, and Prometheus Operator. These advanced techniques ensure that your Prometheus setup is not only robust and scalable but also capable of addressing the complexities of modern, distributed environments.

In this chapter, we provide sample YAML configuration files as guidelines. These examples are not complete configurations; you will need to adapt and modify them with values specific to your environment.

Structure

In this chapter, we will discuss the following topics:

- Secure Prometheus with TLS
- Configuring Long-Term Storage with Remote Write/Read for Prometheus
- Integration with Other Observability Tools
- Capacity Planning and Performance Tuning
- Prometheus Automation Using Operators

Secure Prometheus with TLS

Securing Prometheus with TLS (Transport Layer Security) is crucial to safeguard the sensitive data that it collects and communicates. Prometheus monitors critical systems and services. It collects metrics that include confidential information such as system usage, application performance, and business-critical data points. Without TLS, this information is transmitted in plaintext, making it vulnerable to interception by malicious actors. Encrypting communication with TLS ensures that data remains private and secure during transit.

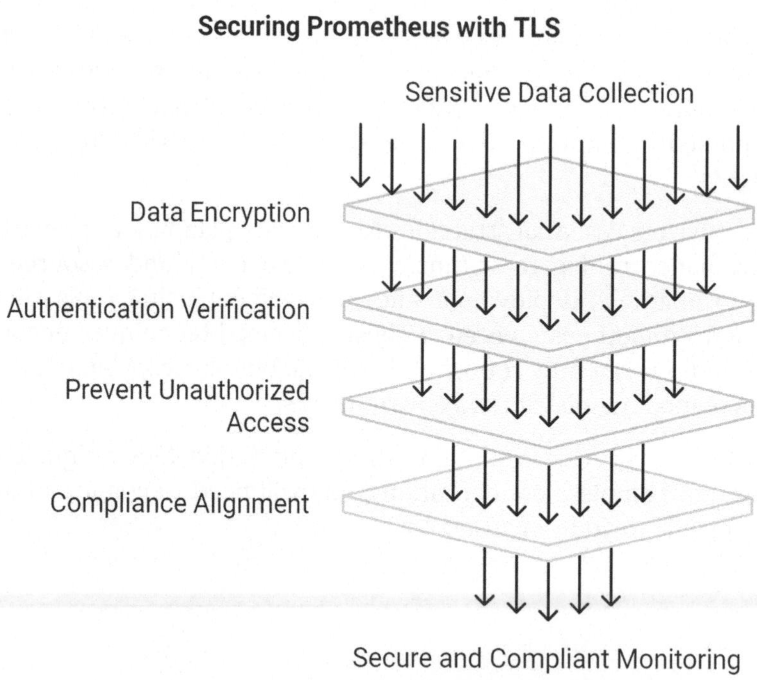

***Figure 9.1**: Securing Prometheus with TLS*

TLS also provides authentication, helping verify the identity of the systems interacting with Prometheus. This prevents unauthorized access and ensures that only trusted clients, exporters, or federated Prometheus servers can communicate with the monitoring system. Without this layer of trust, attackers could inject false data, manipulate metrics, or compromise alerting mechanisms, leading to inaccurate monitoring or missed critical events.

Additionally, securing Prometheus with TLS aligns with modern security standards and compliance requirements, which often mandate encryption for all communication involving sensitive data. This is particularly important for organizations operating in regulated industries such as healthcare, finance, or government.

Given under is a general explanation of the steps needed to secure Prometheus with TLS:

1. **Generate TLS Certificates**

   Before configuring Prometheus, you need to generate or obtain the required certificates:

   - **Server Certificate (`server.crt`)**: Used to authenticate Prometheus to clients.
   - **Private Key (`server.key`)**: A private key corresponding to the server certificate.
   - **CA Certificate (`ca.crt`)**: If you use self-signed certificates, clients will need this CA certificate to validate the server certificate.

You can generate these using OpenSSL or a trusted Certificate Authority. For production use, it is totally recommended that certificates be generated from a trusted certificate authority.

Example commands using OpenSSL:

```
# Generate a private key
openssl genrsa -out server.key 2048
# Generate a Certificate Signing Request (CSR)
openssl req -new -key server.key -out server.csr \
-subj "/CN=<your-prometheus-domain>"
# Create a self-signed certificate
openssl x509 -req -in server.csr -signkey server.key -out server.
crt -days 365
```

Replace **`<your-prometheus-domain>`** with your server's domain or IP address.

2. **Prepare Prometheus Configuration Files**

   Prometheus uses a web configuration file to define TLS settings. This file, often named **`web-config.yml`**, contains the paths to the certificate and key files.

Example `web-config.yml`:

```
tls_server_config:
  cert_file: "/path/to/server.crt"
  key_file: "/path/to/server.key"
```

Replace **`/path/to/`** with the actual paths to your certificate and key files.

Then, In your main Prometheus configuration file (**`prometheus.yml`**), add a reference to the **`web-config.yml`** file under the web section:

```
web:
  config_file: "/path/to/web-config.yml"
```

Here, you need to make sure Prometheus has read permissions for configuration, certificate, and key files.

3. **Restart Prometheus**

   Once the configuration is updated, restart Prometheus to apply the changes. This depends on the way you choose to deploy Prometheus.

   Prometheus will now serve metrics over HTTPS, typically on port 9090 by default.

4. **Validate TLS Configuration**

   Verify the setup by accessing Prometheus over HTTPS in a browser or using tools like *curl*:

   ```
   $ curl -k https://<your-prometheus-domain>:9090
   ```

   - If using a self-signed certificate, include the **`-k`** flag to ignore certificate validation (for testing purposes).
   - For production, ensure the server's TLS certificate is trusted by clients.

5. **Secure Communication Between Prometheus and Clients**

   If Prometheus scrapes metrics from exporters or communicates with **`Alertmanager`** over HTTPS, update the **`scrape_configs`** in **`prometheus.yml`** to include TLS configuration for the targets.

   Example of Scrape Job:

   ```
   scrape_configs:
     - job_name: 'secure-target'
       scheme: https
       tls_config:
         ca_file: "/path/to/ca.crt"     # CA certificate for validat-
   ing the target
         cert_file: "/path/to/client.crt" # Client/Target Certificate
   (optional, in case of enabling Mutual TLS with targets)
   ```

```
      key_file: "/path/to/client.key"  # Client/Target Key
(optional, in case of enabling Mutual TLS with targets)
    static_configs:
      - targets: ['<target-host>:<port>']
```

This setup ensures secure, encrypted communication between Prometheus and its targets.

6. **Enforce Mutual TLS (mTLS)**

   Mutual TLS (mTLS) adds an extra layer of security by requiring both the server and the client to authenticate each other.

   a. **Server-Side Configuration**

      For example, in Prometheus or **Alertmanager**:

   - **Enable Client Authentication**: Update the TLS configuration in **web-config.yml**:

```
tls_server_config:
  cert_file: "/path/to/server.crt"
  key_file: "/path/to/server.key"
  client_auth_type: "RequireAndVerifyClientCert"
      client_ca_file: "/path/to/ca.crt"
```

   This configuration ensures that only clients with valid certificates issued by the trusted CA can communicate with the server.

   b. **Client-Side Configuration**

      For Prometheus to authenticate with an exporter or Alertmanager:

   - Add the client certificate (**client.crt**) and private key (**client.key**) in the **tls_config** section of the scrape or alerting configuration.

Best Practices for Prometheus TLS Communication

Securing communication between Prometheus and its clients is critical to protecting sensitive monitoring data from unauthorized access or tampering. Following these best practices ensures robust encryption, authentication, and overall system integrity:

- **Use Trusted Certificates**: For production environments, always use certificates issued by a trusted Certificate Authority (CA). Trusted certificates are less likely to trigger validation errors and ensure seamless communication between components.
- **Rotate Certificates Regularly**: TLS certificates should be replaced before

they expire to prevent service disruptions. Automating the certificate renewal process using tools such as **Certbot** can simplify this task.

- **Protect Private Keys**: Private keys are the cornerstone of TLS security. Store them in secure locations, such as encrypted directories, and restrict access to authorized users or processes only. Leaked keys can compromise the entire communication setup.
- **Minimize Certificate Scope**: Use unique certificates for different services (for example, exporters, Alertmanager, and Prometheus itself). This limits the impact of a compromised certificate, reducing the risk of cross-service vulnerabilities.
- **Enable Logging**: Enable and review logs for Prometheus and its clients to monitor TLS handshake errors or unauthorized access attempts. Logs provide valuable insights for troubleshooting and detecting potential security issues.

Configuring Long-Term Storage with Remote Write/Read for Prometheus

Prometheus is designed for real-time metrics storage and querying. However, its local storage is limited by disk space and performance constraints, making it unsuitable for long-term metric retention. To address this, Prometheus supports Remote Write/Read, allowing integration with external long-term storage systems. These systems can store metrics indefinitely and enable advanced analysis, large-scale querying, and historical data retrieval.

Reasons for Configuring Long-Term Storage for Prometheus

Long-term storage is essential for overcoming the limitations of Prometheus's local storage, which is not designed to handle massive datasets or retain metrics for extended periods. By offloading data to remote storage, you enable infinite scalability, ensuring that your monitoring system can grow with your needs. It also allows you to retain metrics for years, making it possible to perform in-depth historical analysis, trend forecasting, capacity planning, and meet compliance requirements. Remote storage solutions offer high durability and fault tolerance, safeguarding metrics against data loss due to hardware or software failures. Furthermore, in multi-cluster environments, remote storage centralizes data from multiple Prometheus instances into a single repository, simplifying management and enabling unified querying.

Understanding How Remote Write/Read Works

1. **Remote Write**: Prometheus sends metrics data in real-time to an external storage system via HTTP. This offloads data storage while allowing Prometheus to focus on scraping and alerting.
2. **Remote Read**: Prometheus queries data stored in the external system as if it were local, enabling seamless integration of historical metrics into its ecosystem.

Popular remote storage solutions include **Cortex**, **Thanos**, **Mimir**, and **VictoriaMetrics**. Many of these systems are designed to work natively with Prometheus's remote APIs.

Steps to Configure Remote Write/Read

1. **Set Up External Storage**

   Choose a long-term storage solution that supports Prometheus Remote Write/Read, such as:

   - **Cortex**: Horizontally scalable, designed for multi-tenancy.
   - **Thanos**: Extends Prometheus with global querying and long-term storage capabilities.
   - **VictoriaMetrics**: High-performance and cost-effective for large-scale deployments.
   - **InfluxDB**: Time series database optimized for metrics data.

   Deploy the chosen system and configure its endpoints to accept data from Prometheus.

2. **Configure Remote Write in Prometheus**

   Edit the **`prometheus.yml`** configuration file to enable Remote Write. Add the **`remote_write`** section:

```
remote_write:
  - url: "http://remote-storage.example.com/api/v1/write"
    queue_config:
      capacity: 10000
      max_shards: 200
      max_samples_per_send: 500
    write_relabel_configs:
      - source_labels: [__name__]
        regex: ".*"
        action: keep
```

Where:

a. **url:** Endpoint where Prometheus sends metrics. Replace with your storage system's write API.

b. **queue_config:** Optimizes how metrics are sent. Increasing capacity and max_shards can improve throughput in high-volume environments.

c. **write_relabel_configs:** Controls which metrics are sent to remote storage by applying relabeling rules (for example, filtering or renaming metrics).

3. **Configure Remote Read in Prometheus**

   To query historical data from the external system, add the **remote_read** section:

```
remote_read:
  - url: "http://remote-storage.example.com/api/v1/read"
    read_recent: true
    required_matchers:
      tenant: "production"
```

Where:

a. **url:** Endpoint to query metrics from remote storage.

b. **read_recent:** Allows Prometheus to query recently written data from remote storage if needed.

c. **required_matchers:** Ensures only data matching specific labels (for example, tenant) is retrieved.

4. **Validate Configuration**

   Restart Prometheus and monitor logs for errors related to Remote Write/Read. Check the remote storage system to ensure metrics are being received and stored correctly.

5. **Test Querying Historical Data**

   Use the Prometheus UI or the PromQL query language to test integration. Historical data stored in the remote system should be available alongside local metrics. For example:

```
rate(http_requests_total[1h])
```

This query should include data from both local and remote sources, providing seamless access to long-term metrics.

Best Practices for Long-Term Storage with Remote Write/Read

When using Prometheus with remote write/read for long-term storage, you're extending Prometheus beyond its default short-term in-memory storage by integrating with external systems such as Thanos, Cortex, VictoriaMetrics, InfluxDB, or others.

Here are the best practices to follow for long-term storage using remote write/read in Prometheus:

- **Optimize Write Performance**: Tune **queue_config** settings to prevent bottlenecks in sending metrics to remote storage, especially in high-cardinality environments.
- **Retention Policies**: Use the external storage system's built-in policies to manage data retention, tiering, and deletion, ensuring efficient use of storage resources.
- **Multi-Tenancy Support**: If managing multiple Prometheus instances or environments, choose a storage solution with multi-tenancy features to isolate and manage data efficiently.
- **Data Compression**: Enable compression mechanisms in remote storage to reduce costs and improve storage efficiency.
- **Monitor Write Failures**: Configure alerts on write queue health in Prometheus to detect and resolve issues with Remote Write. For example, alert on increasing queue size or dropped samples.

Challenges and Considerations

- **Query Latency**: Remote Read can introduce latency, especially for complex queries. Solutions such as **Thanos Query** or **Cortex Query Frontend** optimize query performance.
- **Data Consistency**: Ensure synchronization between Prometheus and remote storage during outages or network issues. Most systems handle this via durable write-ahead logs (WAL).
- **Storage Costs**: Long-term storage solutions can incur significant costs. Use efficient compression and query caching to reduce expenses.

Integration with Other Observability Tools

Integrating Prometheus with other observability tools is a common practice in modern DevOps and SRE environments. These integrations help enhance the capabilities of

Prometheus, provide a better context for metrics, and create a unified view of system health and performance.

Reasons for Integrating Prometheus with Other Observability Tools

Following are the key reasons for integrating Prometheus with other observability tools:

- **Enhanced Context**: Prometheus primarily focuses on metrics. By integrating it with tools that handle logs, traces, and events, teams can correlate metrics with other data types, enabling faster and more efficient root cause analysis during incidents or performance issues.
- **Unified Observability**: Combining Prometheus with tools such as Grafana, Jaeger, or Elastic Stack creates a comprehensive view of your system's health and performance. This integration reduces the need to switch between platforms, streamlining workflows and improving operational efficiency.
- **Improved Scalability**: Prometheus's local storage is designed for short-term metrics retention. By integrating Prometheus with long-term storage and analytics tools, you can scale data retention and processing to accommodate larger datasets and longer historical analysis.
- **Automation and Insights**: Integrating Prometheus with AI/ML-powered tools such as Datadog or New Relic unlocks predictive analytics, anomaly detection, and automated alerting. These capabilities enable proactive issue resolution and optimization of system performance.
- **End-to-End Monitoring**: Integrating Prometheus with observability tools for logs and traces provides end-to-end visibility across metrics, logs, and traces. This is especially important for monitoring distributed systems and microservices architectures, where complete observability is essential for maintaining reliability and performance.

Key Integrations for Prometheus

Prometheus can be integrated with a lot of tools, but there are some tools that bring high value when integrated with Prometheus.

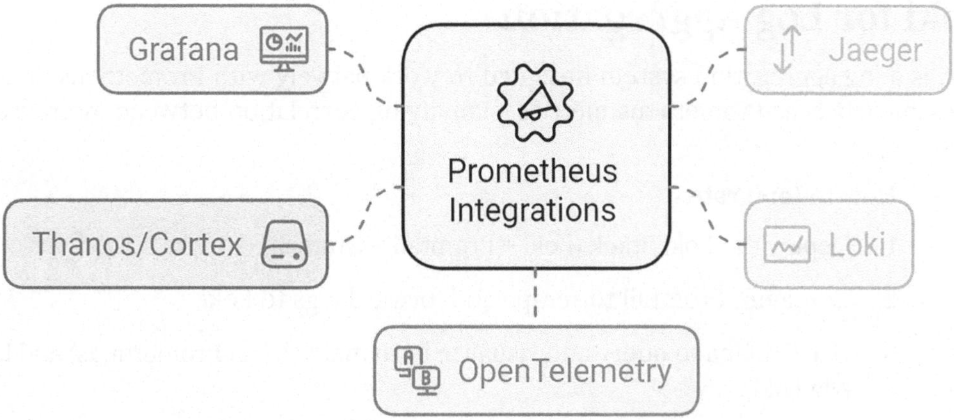

Figure 9.2: *Integrating Prometheus with Other Tools*

Grafana for Visualization

Grafana is the standard for visualizing Prometheus metrics. It provides rich dashboards, query capabilities, and alerts that make data more accessible and actionable.

- **How to Integrate:**
    1. Install Grafana and configure Prometheus as a data source in Grafana.
    2. Use PromQL queries in Grafana panels to display metrics.
    3. Import pre-built dashboards for common use cases such as Kubernetes or node monitoring.

Jaeger for Distributed Tracing

Prometheus provides metrics, but lacks support for distributed tracing. Jaeger traces requests across microservices, helping identify bottlenecks and latency issues.

- **How to Integrate:**
    1. Instrument your application to export traces using libraries compatible with Jaeger (for example, OpenTelemetry).
    2. Use metrics exporters or bridge tools such as `jaeger-query-prometheus` to convert tracing data into Prometheus metrics for unified visualization.

    Example Use Case:

    - Use Prometheus to monitor request rates and errors.
    - Use Jaeger to trace specific slow requests identified in Prometheus.

Loki for Log Aggregation

Loki is a log aggregation system designed to work natively with Prometheus. It uses the same labels as Prometheus metrics, simplifying correlation between metrics and logs.

- **How to Integrate:**
  1. Deploy the Loki Stack (Loki + Promtail + Grafana).
  2. Configure Promtail to scrape and forward logs to Loki.
  3. Use Grafana to query and visualize both metrics (via Prometheus) and logs (via Loki).

Thanos or Cortex for Long-Term Storage

Prometheus's local storage is not suitable for long-term data retention or querying large datasets. Tools such as Thanos or Cortex provide scalable, deduplicated, and distributed long-term storage.

- **How to Integrate:**
  1. Deploy Thanos sidecars alongside Prometheus instances.
  2. Configure Thanos to upload metrics to object storage (for example, S3, GCS).
  3. Use the Thanos Querier for unified, deduplicated querying across all Prometheus instances.

OpenTelemetry for Unified Observability

OpenTelemetry is a vendor-neutral standard for collecting metrics, traces, and logs. Integrating Prometheus with OpenTelemetry provides a unified observability framework.

- **How to Integrate:**
  1. Instrument applications with OpenTelemetry SDKs.
  2. Configure the OpenTelemetry Collector to forward metrics to Prometheus.

Capacity Planning and Performance Tuning

Prometheus can handle substantial workloads, but it requires careful configuration to operate efficiently in large-scale setups. Following are the key areas to focus on:

Adjust Scrape Intervals and Retention Policies

In the following section, you can review how these settings can be adjusted:

Scrape Intervals

Scrape intervals determine how frequently Prometheus collects metrics from targets. Lower intervals provide finer granularity but increase storage usage and resource consumption. For large-scale environments, balance granularity with performance:

- **Critical systems**: Use a smaller interval (for example, 10-30 seconds).
- **Less critical systems**: Use a larger interval (for example, 1-5 minutes).
- **Example configuration**:

```
scrape_configs:
  - job_name: 'critical'
    scrape_interval: 15s
    static_configs:
      - targets: ['critical-service:9090']

  - job_name: 'non_critical'
    scrape_interval: 1m
    static_configs:
      - targets: ['non-critical-service:9090']
```

Retention Policies

Prometheus stores metrics in its time-series database (TSDB). Long retention periods consume significant storage. For large environments:

- Retain only necessary data locally (for example, 15-30 days).
- Offload long-term storage to external systems such as Thanos or Cortex. Example configuration:

```
storage.tsdb.retention.time: 30d
```

Optimize Resource Usage with Proper TSDB Tuning

The Time-Series Database (TSDB) is at the core of Prometheus's storage system. Proper tuning is critical for performance and scalability:

- **Block Size and Duration**: Prometheus writes time series data into immutable blocks. By default, blocks are written every two hours. For high-ingestion systems, increasing this duration reduces write overhead at the cost of higher memory usage during block creation.

Example:

```
storage.tsdb.min-block-duration: 4h
storage.tsdb.max-block-duration: 12h
```

- **Head Block Memory**: The TSDB keeps recent metrics in a "**head block**" in memory before persisting them to disk. Monitor and adjust memory allocation to avoid excessive memory usage:
  - Use the **--storage.tsdb.max-head-chunk-memory** flag to limit memory for head chunks.
- **WAL Tuning**: The Write-Ahead Log (WAL) buffers writes to disk. For high-performance setups, configure the WAL directory on fast storage (for example, SSDs).
- **Cardinality Management**: High cardinality (for example, metrics with too many unique label combinations) can overwhelm Prometheus. Avoid unnecessary labels or overly dynamic label values.

  Example:
  - Bad: **status_code="200, 201, 404, 500"**
  - Better: **status_class="2xx, 4xx, 5xx"**

Use Profiling Tools to Debug Prometheus Performance Bottlenecks

Profiling tools can help identify and resolve performance bottlenecks in Prometheus. Here are common tools and techniques:

1. **Prometheus Built-in Monitoring**: Prometheus itself provides metrics about its performance, which can be queried and analyzed:
   - **TSDB Ingestion Rate:**
     ```
     rate(prometheus_tsdb_head_samples_appended_total[1m])
     ```
   Monitors the number of samples ingested per second.
   - **Query Latency**:
     ```
     histogram_quantile(0.95, rate(prometheus_http_request_duration_seconds_bucket{handler="query"}[5m]))
     ```
   Measures the 95th percentile query latency.
   - **Cardinality:**
     ```
     count(count({__name__=~".+"}) by (__name__))
     ```
   Provides a count of active time series.
2. **pprof Profiling**: pprof is a profiling tool included in the Go programming

language, and Prometheus, being a Go-based application, leverages it for performance analysis. It allows developers and administrators to gather detailed insights into the resource usage of Prometheus, such as CPU, memory, and goroutines. This helps in identifying and resolving performance bottlenecks.

- **How to Enable**: Prometheus's HTTP endpoint exposes profiling data at **`/debug/pprof`**. Enable it during troubleshooting to analyze CPU, memory, and goroutine usage.
- **Profiling Example**:

```
$ curl http://localhost:9090/debug/pprof/profile -o profile.out
go tool pprof profile.out
```

- **Insights**: Use the visual output to identify:
  - CPU hotspots (for example, excessive metric queries).
  - Memory leaks (for example, unoptimized label usage).

3. **PromLens or Prometheus Query Analyzer:** Tools such as PromLens are invaluable for optimizing PromQL queries by detecting inefficient queries that cause high CPU usage and providing suggestions for alternative approaches to improve performance.

Prometheus Automation

Prometheus automation is essential for scaling and managing monitoring systems efficiently, particularly in dynamic environments such as Kubernetes. Automation helps reduce manual intervention, improve consistency, and ensure faster deployments. Here is a detailed explanation of how Prometheus deployment and configuration can be automated:

Automating Prometheus Deployment with Tools like Prometheus Operator in Kubernetes

Prometheus Operator is an open-source Kubernetes operator that simplifies the deployment and management of Prometheus instances in a Kubernetes environment. It provides a more Kubernetes-native approach to manage Prometheus and related components, ensuring the scalability and maintainability of monitoring solutions in Kubernetes clusters.

Key Features of Prometheus Operator:

- **Custom Resource Definitions (CRDs)**: The Prometheus Operator uses Kubernetes CRDs, such as Prometheus, Alertmanager, and ServiceMonitor, to define and manage Prometheus instances, alerting, and scraping configurations.

- **Automatic Configuration Management**: The operator automatically configures Prometheus to monitor services in the Kubernetes cluster based on the defined `ServiceMonitor` or `PodMonitor` CRDs.
- **Scaling Prometheus**: The operator can manage Prometheus scaling by adjusting the number of replicas and setting up persistent storage.
- **Self-healing**: The Prometheus Operator ensures that Prometheus instances are automatically restarted or replaced if they fail, helping maintain high availability.
- **`Alertmanager` Management**: It also automates the deployment and configuration of `Alertmanager`, which is used for alert routing and notification.

Using Prometheus Operator

Step 1: Install Prometheus Operator using Helm or kubectl. You can install it in your Kubernetes cluster with the following Helm command:

```
$ helm install prometheus-operator prometheus-community/kube-
prometheus-stack
```

Step 2: Define Prometheus and Alertmanager CRDs. You can create these resources via YAML files or Helm charts. For example, a basic Prometheus configuration using CRDs would look like this:

```
apiVersion: monitoring.coreos.com/v1
kind: Prometheus
metadata:
  name: prometheus-instance
spec:
  replicas: 2
  serviceMonitorSelector:
    matchLabels:
      team: monitoring
  resources:
    requests:
      memory: "4Gi"
         cpu: "1"
```

This configuration ensures that Prometheus is set up in a Kubernetes environment with automatic scaling and management.

Use Infrastructure as Code (IaC) to Manage Prometheus and Alertmanager

Infrastructure as Code (IaC) allows you to manage and automate infrastructure provisioning, including monitoring tools such as Prometheus and **`Alertmanager`**. By defining infrastructure as code, you can version, share, and replicate your Prometheus setup across environments with consistency and minimal error.

Using IaC Tools for Prometheus Management:

- **Terraform**: Terraform is a popular IaC tool that can be used to define and manage Prometheus configurations and related infrastructure. It works well with cloud-based environments and Kubernetes clusters.
    - **Managing Prometheus Deployment with Terraform**: You can use Terraform to define Prometheus resources such as server instances, alerting configurations, and storage. Terraform modules such as Prometheus can be used to automate setup in cloud environments such as AWS, GCP, or Azure.

Terraform can also be used with Kubernetes to deploy Prometheus and `Alertmanager` by defining Kubernetes resources and automating their management.

- **Helm Charts**: Helm is a package manager for Kubernetes, and **Helm charts** are predefined templates for Kubernetes resources. Helm simplifies the deployment and management of Prometheus and Alertmanager in Kubernetes.
    - **Using Helm to Deploy Prometheus**: Helm charts allow you to configure Prometheus, Alertmanager, and Grafana by providing customizable values through `values.yaml` files. You can adjust the number of replicas, storage settings, and scrape intervals.

  Example Helm Installation:

```
$ helm install prometheus prometheus-community/kube-prometheus-
stack
```

In this case, Helm handles the deployment and configuration of all Prometheus-related components, including Alertmanager, exporters, and dashboards.

Conclusion

This chapter has explored the advanced aspects of Prometheus deployment and management, reviewing the tools and strategies to enhance its functionality and efficiency. We started by discussing how to secure Prometheus with TLS, ensuring encrypted communication and robust authentication mechanisms for your monitoring system. Moving forward, we clarified the configuration of long-term storage using remote write/read capabilities, thus enabling scalable and persistent data retention to meet organizational needs.

Next, we examined integration with other observability tools, showcasing how Prometheus can seamlessly collaborate within a broader monitoring and alerting ecosystem. To address scalability and reliability, we covered capacity planning and performance tuning, empowering you to optimize Prometheus for high-performance workloads. Finally, we highlighted the use of Prometheus operators to automate deployments, upgrades, and configurations, streamlining operational overhead.

In the next chapter, we will review how Prometheus is used across different architectures and real-world applications such as Uber and Soundcloud.

Points to Remember

- Securing Prometheus with TLS ensures that all data transmitted between Prometheus and clients is encrypted, protecting against unauthorized access and data breaches.
- Prometheus can be configured with Remote Write/Read for long-term storage, allowing integration with external databases such as Thanos, Cortex, Mimir, or VictoriaMetrics for storing historical metrics.
- Integrating Prometheus with other tools creates a full observability stack:
  - Grafana for metrics visualization.
  - Loki for logs.
  - Jaeger for distributed tracing.
  - OpenTelemetry for vendor-neutral telemetry data collection.
- Capacity planning in Prometheus involves:
  - Estimating future resource needs based on historical usage trends.
  - Ensuring Prometheus can handle increasing cardinality and data volume.
- Performance tuning includes:
  - Optimizing PromQL queries (for example, avoiding or, reducing cardinality).
  - Scaling Prometheus (for example, sharding, federation).
- Automation tools streamline Prometheus setup and management:
  - Helm for Kubernetes package deployment.
  - Terraform for infrastructure as code.
  - Prometheus Operator for managing Prometheus instances declaratively in Kubernetes.
- YAML configuration examples in this chapter serve as templates – they must be customized to fit the specific use case and environment.

Multiple Choice Questions

1. What is the primary benefit of enabling TLS in Prometheus?
   a. Faster queries
   b. Reducing alert noise
   c. Encrypting communication to secure data
   d. Better Grafana integration
2. Which mechanism allows Prometheus to store historical metrics data beyond its local retention period?
   a. Alertmanager
   b. Remote Write/Read
   c. Grafana Cloud
   d. Log shipping
3. Which tool is typically used for visualizing Prometheus metrics?
   a. Jaeger
   b. Loki
   c. Grafana
   d. OpenTelemetry
4. What does the Prometheus Operator help you manage?
   a. Log collection agents
   b. Alerting rules only
   c. Prometheus setup and lifecycle in Kubernetes
   d. TLS certificates for external services
5. Why is capacity planning important in Prometheus monitoring?
   a. To simplify PromQL syntax
   b. To predict and prepare for future resource needs
   c. To reduce dashboard load times
   d. To collect trace data

6. Which observability tool is most suitable for collecting distributed traces?
   a. Grafana
   b. Loki
   c. Jaeger
   d. Cortex
7. Which tool allows for infrastructure as code and can automate Prometheus provisioning?
   a. PromLens
   b. Grafana
   c. Terraform
   d. kube-proxy
8. What is the main purpose of performance tuning in Prometheus?
   a. Increase memory usage
   b. Encrypt metric data
   c. Improve query efficiency and reduce resource load
   d. Export data to Excel

Answers

1. c
2. b
3. c
4. c
5. b
6. c
7. c
8. c

CHAPTER 10
Prometheus and Real-World Applications

Introduction

In real-world applications, Prometheus demonstrates its value through specific functionalities tailored to each technology domain. In cloud environments, it excels at monitoring native applications and resource utilization, while in microservices architectures, it tracks service health and inter-service communications. For network infrastructure, Prometheus monitors critical metrics such as throughput and latency, while e-commerce platforms benefit from its ability to track transaction processing and user session metrics.

In DevOps environments, it provides crucial insights into build and deployment processes. Across all these applications, Prometheus maintains high scalability, handling millions of metrics efficiently, while offering the reliability and flexibility needed for modern, complex systems.

In this chapter, you will learn about real-world systems and industries where Prometheus plays a vital role in monitoring. We will also highlight the use of Prometheus by some of the largest companies such as Uber and SoundCloud.

Structure

In this chapter, we will discuss how Prometheus shines across the following architectures and real-world applications:

- Prometheus in Cloud Infrastructure Monitoring
    - Role of Prometheus in Supporting Cloud Infrastructure Teams
    - Metrics Provided by Prometheus

- Use Case
- Prometheus in Network Monitoring
  - Role of Prometheus in Supporting Network Teams
  - Metrics Provided by Prometheus
  - Use Case
- Prometheus in DevOps Monitoring
  - Role of Prometheus in Supporting DevOps Teams
  - Metrics Provided by Prometheus
  - Use Case
- SoundCloud Uses Prometheus
- Uber Uses Prometheus

Prometheus in Cloud Infrastructure Monitoring

Modern businesses increasingly rely on cloud infrastructure to support their operations. Cloud environments are dynamic, scalable, and complex, involving a mix of virtual machines (VMs), containers, storage solutions, and managed services. Ensuring the reliability, performance, and efficiency of these infrastructures is crucial for:

- **Uninterrupted Operations:** Downtime or performance degradation can lead to significant revenue loss and damage customer trust.
- **Cost Optimization:** Mismanaged resources can inflate costs, especially in pay-as-you-go cloud models.
- **Scalability:** Businesses need insights to scale infrastructure efficiently based on demand.
- **Compliance and Security:** Monitoring helps meet regulatory standards and detect security anomalies.

Role of Prometheus in Supporting Cloud Infrastructure Teams

Prometheus addresses these needs by providing real-time monitoring, alerting, and detailed insights into cloud infrastructure. Key benefits for IT teams include:

- **Proactive Issue Detection:** Prometheus continuously scrapes metrics from cloud services and underlying infrastructure. IT teams receive early warnings about potential issues, such as CPU spikes, memory leaks, or network congestion.

- **Resource Optimization:** By analyzing utilization metrics, IT teams can identify over-provisioned or underutilized resources, helping reduce costs and improve efficiency.
- **Dynamic Environment Handling:** Prometheus integrates seamlessly with tools such as Kubernetes to monitor dynamic environments, where resources frequently scale up or down. It tracks newly deployed instances automatically.
- **Real-Time Alerting:** Using the Prometheus `Alertmanager`, IT teams receive notifications for critical issues, enabling quick responses to outages or performance problems.
- **Ease of Integration:** Prometheus supports exporters for various cloud services (for example, AWS CloudWatch, Google Cloud Monitoring) and integrates with Grafana for visualizing metrics in dashboards.

Metrics Provided by Prometheus

Prometheus gathers a wide range of metrics to give IT teams a comprehensive view of cloud infrastructure health. Common categories and examples include:

- **Compute Metrics:**
  - **CPU Usage:** Tracks CPU utilization to detect high-load scenarios or idle resources.
  - **Memory Usage:** Monitors memory consumption, helping prevent crashes due to exhaustion.
  - **Disk I/O:** Measures read/write speeds and identifies bottlenecks.
- **Container and Orchestration Metrics:**
  - **Pod Health:** Monitors the status of Kubernetes pods (for example, running, pending, failed).
  - **Node Status:** Tracks the health and availability of nodes in a cluster.
  - **Container Restarts:** Detects containers restarting due to errors.
- **Network Metrics:**
  - **Bandwidth Utilization:** Measures incoming and outgoing traffic.
  - **Latency:** Tracks time delays in data transmission.
  - **Packet Loss:** Identifies issues in network reliability.
- **Storage Metrics:**
  - **Disk Space Usage:** Monitors available and used disk space.
  - **Database Performance:** Tracks query times and connection pool sizes for databases.

- **Service-Specific Metrics:**
  - Prometheus can collect metrics from application-specific exporters such as:
    - **HTTP Latency:** Measures response times for web services.
    - **Error Rates:** Tracks HTTP 4xx and 5xx errors for APIs.

Example Use Case

Consider a company running a high-traffic web application hosted on a Kubernetes cluster. Prometheus can:

- Monitor CPU and memory usage of each container to ensure smooth operation.
- Track network latency to detect slowdowns in user access.
- Alert the team when disk space usage on a node exceeds 80%, preventing potential downtime.
- Provide detailed dashboards via Grafana, enabling real-time visualization of system performance.

Prometheus in Network Monitoring

Networks form the backbone of modern IT infrastructure, supporting applications, services, and user interactions. Ensuring network reliability, performance, and security is crucial for business continuity. Key reasons for implementing network monitoring include:

- **Minimizing Downtime:** Proactive identification and resolution of network issues prevent disruptions in critical services.
- **Optimizing Performance:** Ensuring adequate bandwidth, reducing latency, and preventing packet loss enhance user experience and application performance.
- **Enhancing Security:** Monitoring helps detect suspicious activity or anomalies that may indicate security breaches.
- **Scalability and Resource Management:** Insights into traffic patterns enable informed decisions about network scaling and capacity planning.
- **Compliance:** Adhering to regulatory requirements often involves maintaining detailed logs of network activity and uptime.

Role of Prometheus in Supporting Network Teams

Prometheus plays a vital role in monitoring network infrastructure by providing real-time insights, alerting capabilities, and detailed metrics. Benefits for network teams include:

- **Proactive Issue Detection:** Prometheus continuously scrapes metrics from network devices such as routers, switches, and firewalls. This allows teams to identify and address issues before they escalate, such as high latency or bandwidth saturation.
- **Traffic and Bandwidth Monitoring:** It monitors traffic patterns, helping to optimize resource allocation and prevent bottlenecks. Network teams can identify which devices or applications consume excessive bandwidth.
- **Dynamic Network Monitoring:** In dynamic environments (for example, hybrid cloud setups), Prometheus integrates with service discovery tools to adapt to changes, such as new devices being added to the network.
- **Real-Time Alerts:** Using the Prometheus `Alertmanager`, teams receive instant notifications for critical events, such as network outages, unauthorized access attempts, or configuration anomalies.
- **Integration with Exporters:** Prometheus leverages exporters such as **SNMP Exporter**, **Blackbox Exporter**, and **Node Exporter** to collect metrics from a wide variety of network devices and protocols.
- **Data Visualization:** By integrating with visualization tools such as Grafana, network teams can create custom dashboards to visualize network health, making it easier to analyze trends and spot issues.

Metrics Provided by Prometheus

Prometheus collects a comprehensive range of metrics for network monitoring, including:

- **Traffic Metrics:**
  - **Incoming/Outgoing Traffic (Bytes/Packets):** Measures the volume of data passing through devices.
  - **Traffic Rates:** Monitors bandwidth utilization over time.
  - **Traffic Distribution:** Tracks how traffic is distributed across interfaces or nodes.
- **Performance Metrics:**
  - **Latency:** Measures round-trip time for packets to detect delays.
  - **Throughput:** Tracks the rate at which data is successfully transferred.
  - **Jitter:** Measures variation in latency, which can affect voice and video traffic.

- **Reliability Metrics:**
  - **Packet Loss:** Tracks the percentage of packets that fail to reach their destination, indicating potential network issues.
  - **Error Rates:** Monitors transmission errors, such as CRC errors on physical links.
- **Device Metrics:**
  - **CPU Usage:** Monitors the processing load on network devices.
  - **Memory Usage:** Tracks memory consumption on devices such as routers and switches.
  - **Interface Status:** Reports on whether interfaces are active, down, or experiencing errors.
- **Protocol Metrics:**
  - **SNMP Metrics:** Tracks network status and performance using the Simple Network Management Protocol (via SNMP Exporter).
  - **HTTP/HTTPS Availability:** Monitors web services and APIs using Blackbox Exporter.
- **Anomaly Detection Metrics:**
  - **Unusual Traffic Patterns:** Detects potential DDoS attacks or data exfiltration attempts.
  - **Port Scanning Activity:** Identifies unauthorized attempts to probe network ports.

Example Use Case

A multinational corporation operates a Wide Area Network (WAN) connecting multiple offices, data centers, and remote locations across different regions. The WAN supports critical business applications such as VoIP communication, video conferencing, ERP systems, and data replication. Ensuring high availability, low latency, and minimal packet loss is essential for smooth operations.

Prometheus plays a crucial role in monitoring WAN link performance by collecting metrics such as link utilization, latency, and error rates using an SNMP Exporter, ensuring optimal operation within set thresholds. It enables proactive issue detection through alerting rules for critical conditions such as high latency, packet loss, or bandwidth saturation. By tracking QoS metrics, Prometheus helps prioritize traffic such as VoIP and video conferencing, allowing dynamic adjustments to policies. Integrated with Grafana, it offers real-time dashboards for WAN health, latency trends, and historical data for capacity planning. Additionally, it detects anomalies such as DDoS attacks, unauthorized data transfers, and hardware issues, aiding in security and reliability.

Prometheus in DevOps Monitoring

In modern software development, DevOps and CI/CD pipelines are integral to delivering high-quality applications quickly and reliably. Organizations face the following challenges that make monitoring essential:

- **Ensuring Pipeline Reliability:** Continuous integration and deployment pipelines must function seamlessly to prevent delays in releases.
- **Identifying Build/Deployment Issues:** Failures during builds, tests, or deployments need immediate attention to avoid cascading effects.
- **Optimizing Resource Usage:** CI/CD tools consume compute resources; inefficient usage can lead to performance bottlenecks or increased costs.
- **Tracking Release Quality:** Metrics and monitoring provide insights into the success rates of builds and deployments, helping maintain software quality.
- **Scaling Automation:** As pipelines grow in complexity, monitoring helps DevOps teams to manage automation processes and identify performance issues.

Role of Prometheus in Supporting DevOps Teams

Prometheus empowers DevOps and CI/CD teams by providing comprehensive monitoring and alerting capabilities, ensuring smooth operation of pipelines and supporting faster issue resolution.

- **Monitoring CI/CD Tools and Pipelines:**
    - Prometheus collects metrics from CI/CD tools such as Jenkins, GitLab CI/CD, CircleCI, or ArgoCD using dedicated exporters.
    - Metrics include job status, build times, queue lengths, and resource usage.
- **Proactive Alerting:**
    - Alerts are configured for critical events, such as:
        - Build or deployment failures.
        - Prolonged queue times for jobs.
        - Overloaded agents or nodes in the CI/CD pipeline.
    - These alerts enable teams to address issues before they disrupt workflows.
- **Resource Usage Optimization:**
    - Prometheus monitors resource consumption (CPU, memory, disk I/O) of CI/CD runners or agents, helping teams optimize resource allocation and scale infrastructure as needed.

- **Improving Deployment Reliability:**
  - By monitoring deployment success rates and rollback metrics, Prometheus helps teams identify recurring deployment issues and ensure release stability.
- **Real-Time Insights for DevOps:**
  - Integrations with Grafana provide real-time dashboards to visualize pipeline performance, deployment success rates, and resource usage.
  - DevOps teams gain insights into how different stages of the pipeline (for example, build, test, deploy) are performing.
- **Integration with Observability Ecosystem:**
  - Prometheus integrates seamlessly with other observability tools, such as Jaeger for tracing and Loki for logs, giving a unified view of CI/CD processes.

Metrics Provided by Prometheus

Prometheus collects a variety of metrics to support CI/CD pipelines and DevOps workflows:

- **Pipeline Metrics:**
  - **Job Status:** Tracks whether jobs are successful, failed, or pending.
  - **Build Duration:** Monitors how long each build or deployment stage takes.
  - **Pipeline Success Rate:** Calculates the ratio of successful pipelines to total pipelines.
  - **Job Queue Length:** Tracks the number of jobs waiting to be executed.
- **Resource Metrics:**
  - **CPU and Memory Usage:** Measures the utilization of CI/CD agents and runners.
  - **Disk Usage:** Monitors available and used disk space during builds.
  - **Network Throughput:** Tracks data transfer rates during artifact uploads or downloads.
- **Deployment Metrics:**
  - **Deployment Success Rate:** Monitors how often deployments are completed successfully.
  - **Rollback Frequency:** Tracks the number of rollbacks due to deployment failures.

  - **Version Metrics:** Records which application versions are running in production.
- **Performance Metrics:**
  - **Stage Duration:** Measures the time taken by each pipeline stage (for example, build, test, deploy).
  - **Concurrency:** Tracks the number of parallel jobs being executed.
  - **Error Rates:** Monitors errors during pipeline execution or deployment.
- **Automation Health Metrics:**
  - **Script Execution Times:** Monitors the performance of automation scripts within the pipeline.
  - **Infrastructure Metrics:** Tracks health metrics for CI/CD infrastructure, such as Kubernetes nodes running agents.

Example Use Case

Scenario: A FinTech Company's CI/CD Workflow

A FinTech company uses Jenkins for CI/CD and deploys its applications to a Kubernetes-based cloud environment. Prometheus can:

- **Monitor Pipeline Performance:** Collect metrics on job durations, success rates, and queue lengths in Jenkins to identify bottlenecks.
- **Alert on Critical Failures:** Notify the DevOps team when a critical deployment fails or rollback frequency exceeds acceptable thresholds.
- **Optimize CI/CD Kubernetes Resources:** Track CPU, memory, and disk usage of CI/CD agents running in Kubernetes to prevent resource contention.
- **Visualize Trends:** Use Grafana dashboards to analyze historical build and deployment trends, enabling better capacity planning and process improvements.

SoundCloud Uses Prometheus

SoundCloud, a popular online audio streaming platform, needed a robust monitoring solution to handle the scale and complexity of its microservices-based architecture.

Figure 10.1: *SoundCloud Uses Prometheus as a Monitoring Solution*

The challenges that SoundCloud teams have faced included:

- Monitoring thousands of microservices deployed across multiple data centers.
- Collecting and analyzing metrics in real-time to ensure high availability.
- Proactive issue detection to prevent downtime and maintain a seamless user experience.
- Scaling their monitoring system to match the growth of their infrastructure.

SoundCloud implemented Prometheus to monitor its infrastructure, applications, and microservices. Prometheus became their primary monitoring tool due to its scalability, flexibility, and real-time capabilities.

You can read the following article for more details about how SoundCloud applied Prometheus to resolve series limitations with other tools.

https://developers.soundcloud.com/blog/prometheus-monitoring-at-soundcloud

Uber Uses Prometheus

Uber's rapid growth led to the development of over 4,000 proprietary microservices by late 2014. The existing monitoring tools, Graphite and Nagios, were inadequate for this scale, prompting Uber to seek a more robust solution.

Figure 10.2: *Uber Uses Prometheus as a Monitoring Solution*

The company adopted Prometheus, an open-source monitoring system, to address these challenges. Prometheus's multidimensional data model and powerful query language enabled Uber to effectively monitor its extensive microservices architecture.

To further enhance scalability and meet their specific needs, Uber developed M3, a metrics platform designed to integrate seamlessly with Prometheus. M3 provided a distributed time series database capable of handling billions of metrics, ensuring high availability and global querying capabilities.

Key Features of M3:

- **Scalability:** M3 addresses Prometheus's single-node scalability limitations by providing a distributed time series database, M3DB, capable of handling billions of metrics with long-term retention.
- **High Availability:** The platform ensures continuous monitoring without single points of failure, maintaining data integrity and system reliability.
- **Global Querying:** M3 enables querying across multiple Prometheus instances, offering a unified view of metrics from various sources.
- **Flexible Retention Policies:** It allows for customizable retention and aggregation rules, facilitating efficient storage management and data retrieval.

By open-sourcing M3, Uber contributed to the broader tech community, enabling other organizations to benefit from their scalable monitoring solutions.

For a more in-depth understanding of how Uber introduced M3 as its OpenSource, Large-scale Metrics Platform for Prometheus, you can refer to Uber's case study on the CNCF website (https://www.cncf.io/case-studies/uber/) or Uber's blog (https://www.uber.com/en-NL/blog/m3/#:~:text=Historically%2C%20several%20teams%20at%20Uber,durable%20long%2Dterm%20metric%20store.).

Conclusion

This chapter has demonstrated how Prometheus excels across various domains by providing comprehensive monitoring solutions tailored to the unique needs of different architectures and teams.

The real-world use cases from **SoundCloud** and **Uber** highlight Prometheus' scalability and adaptability. SoundCloud's adoption of Prometheus showcases its ability to handle complex microservices architectures, while Uber's implementation underscores its capability to monitor large-scale, high-traffic systems.

In the concluding chapter of the book, we will discuss the next steps that you can take to certify Prometheus and keep updated with the latest observability technologies.

CHAPTER 11
Conclusion: Future Steps

Introduction

This book covers the foundational exploration of monitoring concepts, emphasizing its critical role in the DevOps lifecycle. It introduces key patterns and anti-patterns to guide effective implementation, along with the technical concepts of Prometheus's pull-based monitoring approach. You would have gained insights into preparing your environments and understanding the interplay between logs and metrics, which sets the stage for Prometheus's practical applications. We then moved to Prometheus's architecture, highlighting its components such as the TSDB, Alertmanager, and Service Discovery, as well as its robust querying capabilities through PromQL. Core metric types such as Counters, Gauges, Summaries, and Histograms were discussed through examples of real-world use cases, offering clarity on selecting the right metrics for their monitoring needs.

The latter part of the book showcases Prometheus's versatility, focusing on practical implementations such as infrastructure monitoring through exporters, dynamic Service Discovery, and advanced techniques such as labeling, relabeling, and storage optimization. A comprehensive overview of alerting mechanisms has been covered to ensure that you can design effective notifications for your systems. Integration with tools such as Grafana and Kubernetes has been discussed to demonstrate how Prometheus fits into a broader observability stack. The penultimate chapter provides real-world use cases, illustrating Prometheus's impact across industries, from cloud infrastructure and microservices to DevOps pipelines and network monitoring. The chapter also outlines the implementation of Prometheus to tackle monitoring challenges by large companies such as Uber and SoundCloud.

This chapter will discuss the next steps that you can take, including certifying Prometheus through the Prometheus Certified Associate (PCA) Exam and being up to date with the latest developments related to Prometheus and its ecosystem.

Structure

In this chapter, we will discuss the following topics:

- Prometheus Certified Associate (PCA) Exam
    - Exam Overview
    - Tips to Pass PCA Exam
- Stay Updated

Prometheus Certified Associate (PCA) Exam

The Prometheus Certified Associate (PCA) Exam is an industry-recognized certification designed to validate foundational knowledge and skills in using Prometheus, an open-source, systems monitoring and alerting toolkit. It is typically targeted at DevOps engineers, system administrators, and developers who use Prometheus for monitoring cloud-native applications and services.

Exam Overview

The PCA exam evaluates the following areas:

- **Core Concepts:** Understanding of Prometheus architecture, including time series data and scraping.
- **PromQL:** Proficiency in the Prometheus Query Language.
- **Configuration:** Configuring Prometheus, including jobs, relabeling, and exporters.
- **Alerting:** Setting up alerting rules and integrating with Alertmanager.
- **Visualization:** Using tools such as Grafana for visualization with Prometheus as a data source.
- **Troubleshooting:** Identifying and solving issues in a Prometheus setup.

Tips to Pass the PCA Exam

1. **Understand the Exam Format**
    - The PCA exam is typically multiple-choice and includes scenario-based questions and practical tasks such as interpreting configurations or PromQL queries.

- Familiarize yourself with the official documentation and any practice tests available.

2. **Master PromQL**
   - PromQL (Prometheus Query Language) is critical. Learn how to:
     - Write queries to extract specific metrics.
     - Use functions such as **`rate()`**, **`sum()`**, **`avg_over_time()`**.
     - Handle aggregations and grouping by labels.
3. **Get Hands-On Experience**
   - Install Prometheus on your local machine or use a Kubernetes cluster.
   - Set up various exporters such as Node Exporter or cAdvisor.
   - Configure scraping jobs, alerting rules, and integrations with Alertmanager.
4. **Focus on Alerting and Integrations**
   - Learn how to write alerting rules.
   - Understand how Alertmanager handles alerts and integrations such as Slack, PagerDuty, or email.
   - Practice writing YAML configurations for these.
5. **Practice Troubleshooting**
   - Familiarize yourself with common Prometheus issues, such as missing data points or incorrect queries.
   - Learn to debug using logs and query results.
6. **Study Key Tools and Concepts**
   - Understand Prometheus's role in observability and how it compares to other monitoring tools.
   - Practice visualizing metrics in Grafana.

More details about the exam, price, and certification agreements can be found through LinuxFoundation (https://training.linuxfoundation.org/certification/prometheus-certified-associate/) or CNCF (https://www.cncf.io/training/certification/pca/) programs.

Stay Updated

Keeping up with the latest developments in Prometheus and its ecosystem is essential for ensuring that your monitoring stack remains efficient and up-to-date. Here is how you can stay informed and adapt to new features and updates:

- **Official Prometheus Resources**
  1. Follow the official blog (https://prometheus.io/blog/) for announcements about new releases, features, and updates.
  2. Check the GitHub releases page (https://github.com/prometheus/prometheus/releases) for detailed information about changes, new features, and bug fixes in every version.
- **GitHub and Open Source Contributions**
  1. Start and watch the Prometheus GitHub repo (https://github.com/prometheus/prometheus) to receive notifications about issues, pull requests, and updates.
     - Explore related projects such as **Alertmanager**, **Thanos**, and **Grafana** for advancements in the ecosystem.
  2. Engage in GitHub discussions or issues to learn directly from developers and contributors.
- **Community Engagement**
  - Prometheus is a CNCF project, so staying active in CNCF webinars, blogs, and conferences helps you stay updated.
  - Participate in Prometheus's community forums, Slack channels, or discussion boards to learn from peers and experts.
  - Attend Prometheus-focused meetups and webinars hosted by the CNCF or local cloud-native groups.
- **Industry News and Blogs**
  - Follow platforms such as DevOps.com, The New Stack, and Medium for articles on Prometheus use cases and updates.
  - Many companies, such as Grafana Labs or observability-focused organizations, publish insights on Prometheus developments.
  - Subscribing to DevOps and observability-focused podcasts or YouTube channels can provide fresh perspectives and tutorials.
- **Experiment with New Features**
  - Keep a test environment to explore new Prometheus features and ecosystem tools before deploying them in production.
  - Participate in beta testing for Prometheus or related tools to gain early exposure to new capabilities.

Index

A

B

C

D

Q

R

S

T

W